CAF

a Loan

A step by step guide for small voluntary organisations

GAIL MOSS

CAF

Published by CAF (Charities Aid Foundation)
Kings Hill
West Malling
Kent ME19 4TA

Editor Rosie Clay

Design and typesetting GreenGate Publishing Services

Cover design Eugenie Dodd Typographics

Cover illustration Emma Dodd

Printed and bound in Great Britain by Bell & Bain Limited, Glasgow

A catalogue record for this book is available from the British Library

ISBN 1-85934-096-2

Telephone +44 (0) 1732 520000
Fax +44 (0) 1732 520001
E-mail cafpubs@caf.charitynet.org
Website http://www.charitynet.org

Contents

About the author 6
Acknowledgements 6
Introduction 7

CHAPTER ONE
What is loan financing? 11
Loan and overdraft facilities 11
Factoring and invoice discounting 13
Asset finance 14
Affinity borrowing 15
Soft lending 18
Secured and unsecured loans 19
Using assets as security 19

CHAPTER TWO
The law relating to borrowing 23
What are your powers to borrow? 23
What rules apply to borrowing? 24
Restrictions for borrowers 29
The law in relation to default 30
Legal aspects of pledging security 32
Seeking independent legal advice 34

CHAPTER THREE
Do you need a loan? 35
Assessing the need for finance 35
Is loan finance the right choice? 36
Productive versus problematic borrowing 38
How much do you want to borrow? 39
Making a business plan 43
The decision to take out a loan 44

CHAPTER FOUR
Where to go for loan finance 47
The lending scene 47
Commercial banks and building societies 48
Charitable trusts and foundations 49
Lenders with a social emphasis 50

CHAPTER FIVE
Choosing a lender 56
How to find a lender 56
What information does the lender need? 59
How to interview the lender 61
Drawing up a shortlist 66
Checklist for choosing a lender 68

CHAPTER SIX
Negotiating a loan 69
How much will you pay? 69
Unexpected costs 74
Making the final decision 75
The lender's formal requirements 76
What happens next? 78

CHAPTER SEVEN
Evaluating your loan 80
Avoiding difficulties 80
Have you made the right decision? 80
When to renegotiate terms 81
Should you extend the loan? 81
Dealing with default 82
Problems with your lender 83

Appendix 85
Useful addresses 86
Useful publications 89
About CAF 90
Other publications from CAF 91
Index 94

Said Paterson:
Hath benefit of interest in all
the moneys which it, the bank, creates out of
nothing.

Ezra Pound, *Unceasing the Measure*

About the author

Gail Moss is a freelance financial journalist writing for national newspapers and magazines on personal finance matters. She has also contributed articles on the financial and legal aspects of running a voluntary organisation to publications for the voluntary sector.

After qualifying as a chartered accountant, Gail worked on contract in Peru, where she then embarked on a career in journalism with locally-based English language publications. She was also BBC World Service correspondent for two years.

Since returning to the UK, Gail has edited *Company Secretary's Review* (from Butterworth Tolley), and was also deputy editor of a monthly magazine for small and growing businesses, both of which gave her an insight into the kind of business issues which are of importance to voluntary bodies.

Acknowledgements

The author would like to thank the following people who have gone out of their way to help in preparing this book: Malcolm Hayday and Mike Hicks of CAF, Doug Burt (currently on secondment to CAF from Barclays Bank), Phil Kilby of Allied Irish Bank, Stephen Lloyd of Bates, Wells & Braithwaite, the Charity Commission, David McGrane of The Co-operative Bank, Christine Goldschmidt of the Hastings Trust (a member of the Development Trusts Association), Malcolm Lynch of Malcolm Lynch Solicitors, Tom Lynch of The Royal Bank of Scotland, Susan Jenkins of Triodos Bank, Penny Shepherd of the UK Social Investment Forum and Nigel Price of Unity Trust Bank.

Introduction

Traditionally, the main force driving the activities of voluntary organisations has been the inflow of money from donors and benefactors. Funds from bequests, individual donations and appeals are spent on running an organisation for its beneficiaries. Some funds may be used to invest in assets which will provide additional income in the future. The guiding principle has always been not to spend money that the organisation does not already possess.

Furthermore, because of its unpaid nature, running voluntary bodies has to a certain extent been the preserve of people who are able and prepared to give their time, such as individuals who are particularly public-spirited, or those who have retired. This has tended to reinforce a fairly conservative approach to financial matters.

However, over the past few years, this attitude has become less helpful. For many voluntary organisations, there is now a gap between their resources and the needs they are trying to meet. This may simply be temporary, such as a delay in receiving grant money. Or it may be more permanent, reflecting the decline in funding on all sides. Government and private grants have generally been cut back, corporate sponsorship is facing pressure from the need to maximise shareholders' returns, and there is severe competition for donations from the National Lottery. At the same time, many individual donors still have a cost-cutting mentality resulting from the last recession. Investment income is already shrinking as companies reduce their dividends because of the abolition of advance corporation tax. Meanwhile, the demands on organisations have grown, as successive governments have shifted responsibility for the provision of care, training and other services from the state to the voluntary sector.

As a result, many voluntary organisations have changed the emphasis of their activities: where once they were campaigning organisations, dependent on donations, they have become social enterprises which provide goods and services for which they can charge fees. Even those which still rely on more traditional sources of income are being forced to consider using commercial financial tools to carry out effectively the activities for which they were set up.

Taking out a loan is one of those tools. A voluntary organisation can borrow money in order to set up a new project which will generate income, or to invest in equipment which will cut costs. On a wider scale, it may need funds to pay for a period of restructuring which is intended to deliver its services more effectively. And at a very basic level, many voluntary organisations can take out a mortgage to buy their premises, giving them security of tenure and a balance sheet asset.

Borrowing can also help a voluntary body achieve its objectives more quickly. Instead of waiting for a lengthy appeal to reach its target, by raising a loan an organisation can start providing its new service, knowing that there will be enough income from the appeal to repay the amount borrowed. Taking out a bridging loan can also remove the worry that an expected grant won't appear before the related bills are due to be paid. More generally, loan finance can help to build a credit history, so that it is easier for the organisation to move on to other business relationships.

Borrowing, however, is not necessarily the only way to bridge a finance gap, and will almost always cost something. So you should always consider the alternatives: providing funds out of your organisation's own cash flow, seeking donations from individuals (possibly from an appeal), and applying for grants from charitable foundations, private companies and the government. It is also worth seeing if you can get funding from the National Lottery Charities Board. These methods of raising finance are described in other books available to the voluntary sector.

How to use this book

This book will guide you through the process of raising loan finance, showing you how to assess your current situation, and looking at the ways in which you can borrow in order to help you run your operation more effectively. The following chapters will:

- explain what the various forms of borrowing are, and how they work;
- tell you how to decide if your organisation needs a loan;
- explain how to obtain a loan;
- explain how to evaluate a loan.

This book is written for anyone with responsibility for running the finances of a voluntary organisation. However, it also includes information on the duties of trustees (members of a board of management if your organisation is not a registered charity). Whether or not you are a trustee yourself, this book will help you to alert the board to their own responsibilities.

The information given is correct at the time of going to press.

CHAPTER 1

What is loan financing?

Loan finance can take many forms, from the obvious loans and overdrafts offered by banks and other financial institutions to more specialist methods, some of which are designed specifically for the voluntary sector. In all cases, loan finance involves borrowing money for a particular purpose; the money is then repaid over an agreed period of time. Usually, interest will be payable and the lender may require some form of security to support the loan.

This chapter describes the main categories of loan, explains how each of them works in practice and discusses when and how loans are secured.

Loan and overdraft facilities

There are two types of conventional lending arrangement – overdrafts and loans.

OVERDRAFTS

An overdraft facility is available only where you have a current account with a bank or other institution. With an overdraft your banker will allow your organisation to go into the red up to an agreed limit. You need to arrange the facility with the bank to begin with (for which an arrangement fee will probably be charged), but once it is set up, you can go overdrawn up to the limit without informing the bank. You pay interest only on the amount by which you are overdrawn. Interest rates are, however, generally higher than for a loan.

Your banker may review your overdraft facility from time to time. The way in which overdrafts work means that they are suitable for covering regular short-term gaps in cash flow. All the main banks now offer them on a case-by-case basis, but there is no guarantee your organisation will get one. You should be aware that for charities, even a temporary overdraft counts as borrowing and leaves trustees open to certain legal liabilities (see Chapter 2).

LOANS

A loan tends to be more suitable where the requirement is for a specific sum of money (say to buy equipment) and your organisation's cash flow is sufficiently predictable for you to plan a repayment schedule.

A separate loan account is opened for a fixed period of between one and 25 years (the longer periods tend to be only for loans to buy property). There are several ways of gaining access to the capital and of repaying capital and interest. The terms are negotiable between lender and borrower; the larger the loan, the greater the scope for arrangements to be tailor-made for the borrower.

If you do not need the whole amount of the loan immediately, you may wish to arrange a 'drawdown' facility which enables you to negotiate a number of different drawings of capital over the loan period. This can be suitable if you are financing a building project. There may also be circumstances where the lender insists on this method to ensure the funds are being spent as intended.

Interest is normally payable regularly on the full amount of the loan, or however much is outstanding once you start to repay it. The most common arrangement for repayment involves the lender periodically (say monthly or quarterly) charging interest to the loan account. The borrower then repays interest and capital by monthly payments.

Variations on how the capital can be repaid, however, may suit different circumstances. You may be able to:

- negotiate a delay in your repayments of capital at the start of the loan;
- pay monthly interest only on the loan with periodic lump sum repayments of capital;
- pay monthly interest and arrange for one 'bullet' repayment of all capital at the end of the loan period. (In this case, and that of lump sum repayments, the lender will need to be certain that the borrower will have the necessary funds. And bullet repayments tend not to be popular with lenders for long-term loans.)

More information on repaying loans is given in Chapter 6.

Factoring and invoice discounting

These financing techniques are commonly used in the commercial sector, but are now also used by a small number of voluntary organisations. They allow you to get sales revenue within a short time of invoicing the customer, rather than waiting for the customer to pay. This then helps your cash flow. The principle involves a factoring or invoice discounting company paying your organisation a percentage of your unpaid invoices, up to a specified limit, say 85 per cent. Then, as the debts are cleared, it pays you the remaining 15 per cent, less its charges. With an invoice discounting service, you chase up your own debts and then pay the invoice discounters as your own receipts come in; with factoring, the company does all the collection for you, paying any balance over to you once the money is in.

However, these facilities are not suitable for most voluntary organisations. They are really only appropriate if your organisation is selling services. But even then, they can only be used where your debts are assignable, ie the ownership of the debts can be passed on to another organisation. Unfortunately, most organisations selling services are dealing with clients such as local authorities who issue standard contracts which are not assignable. If this is the case with your organisation, it is still worth asking your clients if the contracts can be rewritten to allow the debt to be assigned.

If you want more information, your clearing bank may well have a commercial finance arm which offers this type of service. Alternatively, you can get a list of invoice discounting and factoring companies from the Factors & Discounters Association (see Useful addresses).

Asset finance

Hire purchase and leasing – otherwise known as asset finance – are forms of borrowing which allow an organisation to use an asset even though it has not been fully paid for. This type of borrowing can be used for assets such as plant and machinery, office equipment, agricultural equipment and business cars.

Both types of arrangement last for a fixed period over which your organisation makes regular payments to the finance company, which buys the equipment on your behalf. The period often lasts for the asset's natural lifetime – with a car, for instance, this might be two or three years, after which time you might want to change the vehicle.

The main difference between the two forms of finance is that with hire purchase, your organisation eventually becomes the legal owner of the asset, provided you have paid all the instalments and the option to purchase fee. This change of ownership generally takes place at the end of the agreement, but it might, exceptionally, occur beforehand, depending on the terms of the individual agreement. For this reason, you can claim capital allowances (this is obviously important for the trading subsidiaries of charities). These can be claimed right from the start of the agreement.

With leasing, the payments are considered to be the cost of renting the asset, so you will never in fact own it. However, the finance company can claim capital allowances and pass on the benefit to you, via reduced rental charges. Furthermore, as the asset always belongs to the finance company, it can act as security for the financial arrangement. You may therefore be offered slightly better terms than you would get from other lenders.

Whichever type of arrangement you choose, you will normally be responsible for maintaining the equipment for the duration of the agreement, although with some deals, such as the contract hire of vehicles, the leasing company does take some responsibility, for instance paying for repairs and replacement parts.

More information about asset finance is available from the Finance & Leasing Association (see Useful addresses), who can also supply a list of members.

Affinity borrowing

Voluntary organisations can try to raise money by making an affinity borrowing relationship with a bank. Affinity borrowing means a long-term, committed relationship between the voluntary organisation and the institution it is borrowing from. With this kind of arrangement, the lender may be willing to allow the organisation more leeway because of its social objectives. Affinity borrowing can also mean that the organisation borrows from its supporters. Generally speaking it is the banks operating with a social emphasis which offer affinity borrowing, although commercial banks may do so in very specific circumstances.

There are several ways in which this type of relationship can work.

AFFINITY SAVING AND LENDING

Under an affinity saving and lending scheme the bank sets up accounts for savers who want their deposits to fund specific projects or sectors. The savers may choose to forego some or all of their interest in order to support those areas. The leader in this type of lending is Triodos Bank, and there is more information on this in Chapter 4 (see page 53).

GUARANTEE COMMUNITIES

Many organisations, especially the smaller ones, have problems because they have no security to offer the lender – they may, for instance, rent their premises and therefore cannot offer the property. But if organisations have a strong supporter base, or a high level of social and community interest in their activities, they may be able to turn it into banking collateral by using a guarantee community. This technique is particularly common amongst the banks operating with a social emphasis. By this means, supporters of an organisation can give guarantees to secure a loan, as the case study below illustrates.

Using a guarantee community, however, does not remove the need for a secure source of repayment. The technique could, for example, be used to guarantee bridging finance when the organisation is waiting for a grant.

CASE STUDY

An urban regeneration charity planned to set up a small social history centre in an inner city area suffering from planning blight. It had to wait two years from applying for EU grant money to actually receiving the funds. The amount of the grant was to be £30,000, and after taking into account income from its activities, the charity needed a loan of £25,000 for two years, to cover the income shortfall. The total interest payments were calculated at £2,000, giving a total of £27,000 to be repaid to its bank. The charity found about 60 supporters who were each willing to give guarantees of between £250 and £1,000. On this basis, and complying with the bank's other requirements such as an adequate business plan, the charity was successful in obtaining the loan finance.

However, a potential drawback is that calling on guarantees will probably damage the relationship between the organisation and its supporters, so it is vitally important to establish a programme for repaying the money.

BORROWING COMMUNITIES

This is another borrowing technique which can be offered by social lenders. It can be used to fund a small discrete project or to fill a gap in the whole fundraising programme, because it means that work can begin immediately, rather than waiting for donations which will come in at irregular intervals. It is generally used for small amounts – a typical scenario might be the start-up of a project where most of the money has already been raised from gifts, but where there is a shortfall which can be met over the years by income from supporters' donations.

A group of the organisation's supporters gets together to form a borrowing community which takes out the loan. The capital sum is given to the organisation, but the borrowing community has the responsibility of repaying it. The individual members of the borrowing community each make small regular repayments, and their repayments are themselves guaranteed by others.

However, if you are considering this method of providing finance, you should be aware of the implications under the Financial Services Act (from summer 2000, the Financial Services and Markets Act). Although a borrowing community involves a form of giving, if you think it might be seen as an investment advertisement you should contact the Financial Services Authority's (FSA) Public Enquiries Unit (see Useful addresses) to get guidance on your individual circumstances.

It is possible that setting up this arrangement could also be seen as deposit-taking under the Banking Act 1987. In this case you either have to become an authorised deposit-taker with a licence from the FSA or you have to get exemption. Ideally, you need specialist legal advice, but a good start would be to contact the FSA Public Enquiries Unit for general guidance. A list of the current exemptions under the Act is given in the Banking Act 1987 Exempt Transactions Regulations 1997 (Statutory Instrument 817) available from the Stationery Office (formerly HMSO – see Useful addresses).

Soft lending

A 'soft' loan is lent on more favourable terms than normal commercial lending, for instance at below commercial rates of interest or with repayment holidays. This type of lending may be available from both commercial banks – who sometimes shave a fraction off the interest rate margin they would charge to a commercial borrower – and from lenders with a social emphasis. The 'social' lenders may, for instance, charge lower rates if they are running targeted deposits where the depositor accepts a lower rate of interest because their money is being used for a particular project or sector (see page 53).

However, although soft lending may be attractive from your point of view as a borrower, you should not spend too much time looking specifically for that kind of arrangement. If you are prepared to agree to more conventional terms with a mainstream lender, you'll have more choice from which to pick the right package. In any case, there are ways you can make the terms easier – you can, for instance, lower your monthly repayments by extending the term of the loan, although this of course will mean you incur more interest in total.

Secured and unsecured loans

Most lenders want some sort of back up which ensures they will still get their money back even if the borrower is unable to repay the loan or the related interest. The most common way to do this is to 'secure' the loan on assets owned by the borrower. This means the lender has the right to legal ownership of the asset (or title to the asset, in lawyers' language) if the borrower goes into default, ie breaks one of the conditions of the loan agreement. The most obvious example would be if the borrower stopped making repayments. Most loans to voluntary organisations are on a secured basis. Where an asset has been promised as security in this way, it is described as 'charged'.

However, lenders may sometimes be willing to advance the money without demanding any security. Institutions which lend to the voluntary sector are often prepared to do this, but these days some of the commercial lenders such as the banks may also offer loans without security. For instance, if you have run a current account with your bank for a number of years, have a secure flow of income and know that the bank is happy with the way your organisation is managed, you may be able to borrow without charging any assets, as long as the bank is happy that your project makes financial sense. In this case the loan is described as unsecured.

The ways in which different types of asset can be used as security are described below. However, it's important to remember that once you've pledged a specific asset as security for a loan, it may not be possible to use it as security for other borrowing; some lenders refuse to accept property if it already has a charge over it.

Using assets as security

While all the assets listed below enable the lender to offer funds knowing the assets can be sold if the debt is not repaid, they also place a limit on the amount which you can borrow. For instance, a lender will only advance a certain percentage – say 70 per cent – of the value of a property. The percentage is called the 'loan-to-value ratio'. The ratio varies according to the type of asset used as security, and the individual lender. So one lender might give you up to 80 per cent on property, 25 per cent on machinery and equipment and 40 per cent on book debts, while another might advance 75 per cent on property, 20 per cent on plant and equipment and 45 per cent on book debts.

PROPERTY

This is the type of asset most commonly used to secure borrowing by voluntary organisations. The property will either be freehold, where your organisation owns the property outright, or leasehold, where you have acquired the rights to occupy a property for a specified number of years. The terms of leases vary. For instance, a lease on a residential property could run for a period up to 99 years, or on a commercial property, the lease may be shorter with a fixed rent reviewed on a seven-year basis.

As a rule, lenders do not like the shorter commercial leases – that is those with twenty years or less to run – because a fixed rental agreement has little value unless rents generally shoot up. Even if your organisation owns the freehold, there may be a problem with property which has a specialised use – for instance, a church hall – and which might therefore be difficult for the lender to sell.

If your organisation does agree a charge on its property, the charge must be registered with the Land Registry.

MACHINERY AND EQUIPMENT

If your organisation's operations involve manufacturing, you may be able to offer the machinery as security. Whatever your activities, however, you may be able to use office furniture and equipment such as PCs and fax machines, although this type of security is not really attractive to lenders, since it has a very low resale value. And the office equipment may already have 'walked' by the time the lender starts to call in the loan. You may be able to secure loans on vehicles owned by your organisation – for instance, buses or coaches if you provide transport for your beneficiaries. Again, however, it is difficult to find buyers for second-hand passenger vehicles – bus companies prefer to buy new ones.

BOOK DEBTS

It may be possible for a lender to take a floating charge (see page 33) over your organisation's book debts, which are amounts owed and unpaid, for instance, for services delivered. The lender is only likely to consider this if it feels your organisation is well-managed and you have a good prospect of collecting the debts. However, if things go wrong with your loan and the lender calls in these debts, it can be tricky for the lender to get the money back, because once the debtors realise your organisation is in difficulties, they may reckon they can get away without paying up. So this is not a popular form of security.

EU CONTRACTS

Your organisation may be carrying out contracts on behalf of EU agencies, for instance providing educational services to Eastern Europe. These will be paid for in arrears, so the payments due are, in effect, assets which can be used to secure a loan. However, the main problem with using them is that there is no guarantee of payment until the client (ie the EU agency) has agreed that the work has been satisfactorily carried out, and this often occurs only when the organisation is actually paid. Without this acknowledgement of the debt, it is unlikely to be attractive as security. Furthermore, EU agencies tend to be slow payers. It will be easier to get the lender to accept these contracts as security if your organisation has established a successful track record of completing contracts.

STOCK MARKET INVESTMENTS

In some cases, you may be able to give a charge on the stocks and shares which your organisation holds, as long as they are quickly realisable. However, there are several problems:

- Lenders may be unwilling to use an asset which could reduce in value if the market falls just when the lender wants to call on the security.
- It may not be possible to use holdings in pooled investments, such as common investment funds, because the fund managers may be unable to identify which specific holdings belong to your organisation.
- You may be unable to use funds held on permanent endowment. You would certainly have to check with the trust deed of the endowment as to whether or not it expressly forbids you from using these investments as security.

CHAPTER 2

The law relating to borrowing

Borrowing money inevitably means that your organisation is taking on some financial risk, and because of that a network of rules and regulations exists to protect both borrowers and lenders. It is therefore crucial to be aware of what restrictions there are to avoid running foul of the law. This chapter explains the legal responsibilities of both parties to a loan, concentrating particularly on the legal powers voluntary organisations have to borrow.

What are your powers to borrow?

THE GOVERNING DOCUMENT

Before you even start considering taking out a loan you need to find out whether or not your organisation has the power to borrow. Any prospective lender will want to know you have this power, and this applies to overdrafts too. To establish this, you need to see whether the power to borrow is expressly contained in your organisation's constitution. If your organisation is a trust you need to look at the trust deed. A registered company should consult its Memorandum and Articles of Association.

If there is no express power to borrow, there may be an implied capacity in law. For example, with some corporations, such as those with a Royal charter, anything that is not specifically banned from their constitution can be carried out. You may need to get professional advice on whether your organisation falls into this category.

If your organisation does not possess the power to borrow, you should consider whether you can amend its constitution to allow it to do so. In this case, you will need a power of amendment. That may sound obvious, but there are many badly drafted constitutions which do not contain one. If your organisation is a charity, you will need to go to the Charity Commission (see Useful addresses) for a scheme to amend your constitution to allow you to borrow. Don't assume that you will automatically get it; you may have to justify to the Commission that your proposed borrowing is a reasonable and sensible thing for the trustees to do.

What rules apply to borrowing?

CHARITIES ACT 1993

The following rules apply in law to registered charities. However, even if your organisation does not have charitable status, they do form a guide to best practice.

Justifying the decision to borrow

Charity trustees are under a general duty to act always in the best interests of the charity, and that applies just as much to borrowing money as to any other situation. So while, as individuals, they might be willing to take a slight gamble with their own money in the hope of making gains, they cannot take the same risks with assets which belong to the stakeholders in the charity, such as beneficiaries and donors.

The trustees therefore need to weigh up very carefully what the benefits are of borrowing, compared with the disadvantages. It is crucial for them to have a very clear set of board minutes containing the resolution to borrow which explains the reasons for doing so. These reasons should include why the organisation needs the money, why the trustees have decided to borrow (as opposed to getting other forms of funding), and why this particular form of borrowing has been chosen. The minutes might also, for instance, explain why a specific rate of interest was agreed with a lender in relation to the prevailing economic conditions. If there are some relevant background documents, these should be annexed to the minutes and kept.

In deciding on an arrangement with a particular lender, trustees should also have taken steps to protect themselves by getting competitive quotes from several sources (more information about this is given in Chapter 5, see page 56).

It really is important to gather as much evidence as you can to back up the trustees' decision. If things go wrong with the borrowing later on, you are certainly going to be asked why you decided to do it, and if you have no evidence to back up your decision, your trustees could be made to look rather negligent.

CASE STUDY

A charity providing support and accommodation for homeless people in a run-down area of town wanted to buy its own property in order to expand its activities and bring in more income. The property had to be in the specific locality where it operated, as this was where most of its clientele were living.

The charity approached several lenders, all but one of whom refused loan facilities because of the uncertainty of the charity's income stream; the charity was waiting for the results of some grant applications but did not have any physical security, apart from the property it hoped to buy.

One lender was receptive, and eventually made an offer of a variable rate (11 per cent), which was around two per cent above the then market norm of nine per cent. The charity had to decide whether to take the loan, or to wait a year or two until its grant funding was sorted out, and hope to get a mortgage at lower rates.

However, the local council had just approved a redevelopment scheme nearby, which the charity trustees expected would increase property prices in the surrounding area. They took advice from local surveyors and were told that prices could rise by as much as 20 per cent in the next two years. If that were to happen and they took out a loan further down the line, they would be paying just as much interest, even with a lower rate, because the principal sum would be correspondingly higher.

The trustees decided to go ahead with the loan. They prepared full back-up documentation including the surveyors' assessment, copies of the planning permission from the local council, and a memo from their operations manager as to why it was important for the charity to be based in that particular locality. So even if the redevelopment scheme did not go ahead, or property prices did not go up as expected, the trustees could still prove they had cogent reasons for taking out an expensive loan.

Approval of the Charity Commission

Whether or not a loan is secured, a charity can go ahead without the approval of the Charity Commissioners as long as the charity has obtained and considered proper advice, in writing. This must cover:

- whether the proposed loan is necessary in order to pursue the desired course of action;
- whether the terms of the loan are reasonable;
- the charity's ability to repay the loan on the terms arranged.

The charity trustees must reasonably believe the person giving the advice to be qualified and experienced in financial matters, and the person must have no financial interest in making the loan, although they can be an officer or employee of the charity.

However, the consent of the Charity Commission is needed if the lender is a 'connected person' (see page 28 for a definition). To obtain consent, the trustees or solicitors should contact the Charity Commission giving all the relevant information. The procedure normally takes two or three weeks.

This does not apply, however, if the lending involves a mortgage over land, or land and buildings, and the authority to take out a mortgage is contained in an Act of Parliament, a statutory instrument, or a Scheme of the Court of the Commissioners. The Charity Commissioners publish a useful booklet *Acquiring Land* (CC33) which gives more information on the relevant rules (see Useful publications).

Obtaining financial advice

Whether or not the lending is secured, the trustees must by law obtain and consider the advice of someone whom they reasonably believe has sufficient ability in, and practical experience of, financial matters to give them sound advice. This can be an officer or employee of the charity, but whoever it is, they must not have any financial interest in the loan.

This person must provide the trustees with written advice on three issues:

- whether the loan is necessary in order for the trustees to be able to pursue the particular course of action for which they are seeking loan finance;
- whether the terms of the loan are reasonable;
- the charity's ability to repay the loan on the terms agreed with the lender.

If trustees do not obtain advice on matters on which they are not themselves experts, they could be seen as having acted imprudently, and may be personally liable for the consequences. This also applies to borrowing in forms such as a temporary overdraft.

This all sounds quite obvious, but it can sometimes happen in practice that the organisation has a senior employee who suggests a particular course of action, and assures the trustees or directors that advice has been taken. It may be tempting for the board to accept this on trust, but the trustees should always ask to see what advice the employee has in fact received. If it has only been given verbally, they should ask for the advice to be put in writing, addressed to themselves rather than the employee. This means that the person giving the advice knows that it is going to be seen by the trustees.

If the trustees are for some reason unable to get the appropriate advice, they should ask the Charity Commission for their consent. The Commission publishes the booklets *Responsibilities of Charity Trustees* (CC3) and *Responsibilities of Trustees: A Summary* (CC3(a)) which have useful guidelines on the general duties of trustees (see Useful publications).

Who is a 'connected person'?

As with any other institution, there could be a conflict of interest if a charity carries out a commercial transaction (such as a loan) with someone within the organisation, or who otherwise has some connection with it. So the Charities Act 1993 lays down a definition of so-called 'connected persons' and sets out restrictions on what they can and cannot do in relation to the charity concerned. A connected person falls into at least one of the following categories:

- a trustee of the charity;
- a person who is the donor of any land to the charity;
- a child (including a stepchild and an illegitimate child), parent, grandchild, grandparent, brother or sister of any trustee or donor;
- an officer, agent or employee of the charity;
- the spouse of any person falling within any of the above categories;
- an institution which is 'controlled' by any of the above people, or any two or more of the above together. ('Controlling' an institution means being in a position where you can get it to act as you wish);
- a corporate body in which any connected person has a substantial interest, or two or more such people have a substantial interest.

BORROWING BY A TRADING COMPANY

Sometimes, if a charity has a trading subsidiary, the subsidiary needs to borrow to finance its operations. If it has no assets, the banks may be reluctant to take on the risk, so the solution may appear to be for the parent charity to borrow money which in turn is loaned to its trading company. However, doing this may mean the charity risks losing a number of tax exemptions. To avoid this (provided the loan is for the benefit of the charity and not for tax avoidance) the trustees can make a formal claim, ie in writing, under Schedule 20 of the Income and Corporation Taxes Act 1988 to the Financial Intermediaries and Claims Office (FICO) (see Useful addresses). The FICO can also informally assess a transaction before it is made. In addition, trustees should also get professional external advice.

Restrictions for borrowers

Normally, loan agreements are widely cast in the lender's favour. Some of the restrictions on borrowers are as follows:

- There are usually restrictions on what borrowers can do with the loan funds. If the borrowing is for a specific purpose, there is usually a covenant (ie an undertaking to comply with certain conditions) with the lender to apply the money for particular purposes or usage, such as buying computer equipment or refurbishing a building.
- If the loan is to buy property, the borrower may have to undertake to insure the property adequately, and make sure the value of the insurance cover is maintained. The lender will want evidence that the premium is maintained and cover adequate.
- The agreement often contains 'negative pledges' ie promises not to allow certain things to happen. For instance, the organisation may promise that its profits (surplus if it is a charity) will not fall below £X,000 per year, or that the value of its assets will not go below £Y million. There can also be 'positive pledges' such as the promise to supply the lender

with quarterly management accounts within a month of the end of the relevant quarter. If the pledge is broken, the borrower is technically in default and the lender can start legal proceedings to get its money back.

- The lender may commit itself to drip-feed the money out only when it has seen invoices, such as architects' certificates, as proof that what is being financed has actually been bought, and as reassurance that the security exists.

The law in relation to default

If an organisation cannot repay the loan or the related interest, what happens next depends on whether the organisation has limited or unlimited liability. If it is set up as a limited liability company, a company limited by guarantee, an industrial provident society, or an organisation incorporated by Royal Charter or by Act of Parliament, it will have limited liability. On the other hand, trusts and unincorporated associations do not have limited liability.

ORGANISATIONS WITH LIMITED LIABILITY

If the borrowing is made by an incorporated organisation with limited liability, then its liability is limited to its assets. So if, for instance, it borrows a million pounds, and its assets turn out to be worth only £200,000, the organisation's creditors lose the £800,000 difference.

ORGANISATIONS WITH UNLIMITED LIABILITY

If a loan is made to an unincorporated trust, the trustees' names appear on the loan documentation. The key fact to understand here is that the loan is the personal responsibility of the trustees unless the trustees have contracted out of liability (see below). If the trust's assets are not enough to meet the liabilities, the trustees could be sued personally by the lender – so, for instance, personal assets such as their home could be at risk. They could even, in theory, be made bankrupt.

If an unincorporated association takes out the loan, again it is the members of the management committee who could get sued if the loan cannot be paid off. However, depending on how the constitution is worded, they may have an indemnity from the members of the association who elected them to serve on the management committee. Many unincorporated associations have a membership greater than those people who serve on the committee. Trustees of a trust, however, cannot seek indemnity because a trust does not have a membership – an unincorporated association does.

CASE STUDY

The management committee of a cricket club agreed to borrow £250,000 to refurbish the pavilion, including setting up a function room facility. The loan was secured on the property, but the bank pointed out to the committee that if the loan was not repaid, it might not be able to realise the full amount by selling the pavilion, because of its specialised use and because the ground (which was leased from the council) could not be sold for development.

So the management committee asked for an equal indemnity from all the members of the association. There were 500 members, so each was liable to pay up to £500 if the club failed to repay the loan.

CONTRACTING OUT OF LIABILITY

By agreement with the lender, an unincorporated trust or unincorporated association can limit its liability. When the loan is arranged, the lender agrees to limit its claim in the case of default to the value of the trust's or association's net assets. This way, the lender will have no claim whatsoever against the trustees personally except in the case of misrepresentation or fraud. So if your organisation is unincorporated, you should see if you can get this kind of provision written into the lending agreement to act as an effective limitation of liability, by contract. Whether a lender will accept this, however, probably depends on how much money is being advanced and how the lender assesses the security your organisation can provide.

INSOLVENCY

Insolvency is relatively uncommon in the voluntary sector, but if a loan is defaulted on because the borrower has gone to the wall, then there will be several creditors – not just the lender – who want to be paid out of the borrower's assets (if any). Precisely how these assets are used to pay creditors depends on how the voluntary organisation is constituted and the priority of the creditors. For instance, different arrangements apply to a limited liability company than to an industrial provident society. If there are assets to be used, a receiver or a liquidator will deal with matters; if not, the Department of Trade and Industry will be brought in to sort out the situation.

Legal aspects of pledging security

Security for a loan can take several forms (see page 19). In all cases, however, from a legal perspective, the central point concerns the ownership of the asset offered as security. If your organisation defaults on a loan, the lender can choose to exercise their right to the ownership of the asset to pay back the debt.

CHARGES, MORTGAGES AND DEBENTURES

When lawyers are talking about security for loans, they often use three words interchangeably – charge, mortgage and mortgage debenture – which can be very confusing for laypeople. In fact, these words mean slightly different things.

- **A charge**, as explained in Chapter 1 (page 19), is an arrangement whereby legal ownership of an asset is offered to someone else as security for a loan or to meet some other liability. Legal ownership remains with the original owner unless conditions of the charging agreement are not met. In this case, the lender can exercise their right to the ownership of the asset and dispose of it to realise the amount owed.

A charge can be fixed, or floating. If the charge is fixed, this means that it applies to particular assets of a fixed nature such as a building or land, but you can also have a fixed charge over an asset that changes in value, such as debtors, equipment and machinery.

A floating charge hangs above a class of asset which is constantly coming in and out, such as stock. The charge comes into play when a specified event – called the crystallisation event – occurs. This takes place usually when the borrower defaults on the debt, for example when interest or capital payments are not made on a due date, and the lender decides to call in the loan. At this point, the charge 'crystallises' and drops like a net, capturing everything in that asset class at that moment. If the charge is over stock, for example, all the stock in the warehouse that day suddenly becomes charged to the lender. This means the lender or receiver (if one has been appointed) can then sell it.

- **A mortgage** is a particular type of charge which relates to land and property.
- **A mortgage debenture** is a charge or mortgage over all the assets of a limited company.

IF SECURITY IS CALLED IN

If a secured loan is defaulted on, as has already been stated, under the terms of the loan agreement the lender can dispose of the assets given as security to repay the debt. Usually, the lender does this by serving notice. In these circumstances, whoever has the charge can take out of the proceeds only the money they are owed (plus accrued fees and interest) – the rest goes back to the original owner or to the receiver to pay other debts. If several classes of asset are charged, the lender can choose which ones to exercise his or her rights over.

You should also be aware that even if your borrowing facility is unsecured, there is still some risk attached. If your organisation defaults, it can be sued by the lender. If the lender succeeds in getting a judgement against your organisation in the courts, the lender could then have access to the organisation's property, such as its bank balance.

Seeking independent legal advice

If you're taking out a loan, you should *always* seek legal advice. You need to be able to understand the loan document, and your organisation's rights within it. This is particularly important with secured lending because of the legal complications which are involved. If a loan involves a mortgage over your organisation's assets, there will be a complicated mortgage document, which you also need to understand. Often, too, the interest provisions can be very complicated.

Because of the specialised nature of the voluntary sector, it is best to get advice from a solicitor with relevant experience. Not only does this lessen the chances of your being given the wrong advice, it also means you're not paying for their learning time. You could, of course, use your existing solicitors. Failing that, professional firms looking for business in the voluntary sector feature in the regular listings and annual surveys produced by trade publications such as *NGO Finance* and *Charity Times* (see Useful addresses).

CHAPTER 3

Do you need a loan?

This chapter aims to help you think about why your organisation needs additional finance and whether taking out a loan is the best way forward. Advice is included on the practical steps you will need to take, such as deciding how much to borrow, preparing a business plan and how to take out the loan itself.

Assessing the need for finance

In an ideal world, voluntary organisations would be able to pay for everything out of their normal income, whether this was from donations, special fundraising efforts, grants or fees for services. Unfortunately, of course, this state of affairs is not easy to achieve. You may be aware that you are struggling to fulfil all your objectives or, worse, that you are not able to meet your planned commitments. But before you start looking for additional income from any source, you need to examine carefully what your financial needs are, as these will help determine the most appropriate methods of funding:

Look at your flow of income and expenditure over the last year and compare it with previous years.

- Have certain types of income fallen away? If so, how could you replace them?
- Have your overheads increased? Is there room for greater efficiency or cost cutting?
- Has the demand for your services risen whilst income has remained stable?
- Are there temporary gaps in your organisation's income stream, perhaps because you have to wait to receive a promised grant?

Look closely at your sources of income.

- Are you receiving as much money as you could from these sources? With relatively little extra effort it may be possible to adjust existing arrangements to increase your income, for instance by persuading your donors to covenant their gifts.

Consider your present and future commitments in the context of your overall objectives.

- Do you need more money in order to restructure so that you can deliver your services more effectively?
- Do you need a new building, premises, equipment or staff training to meet a rising demand for your services?
- Is there some other new development which your present source of income will be inadequate to meet?

What is clear from the above questions is that a loan will not necessarily be the best solution to all types of financial problems, particularly those of a recurrent nature. So it is important that your organisation considers all the options before deciding on loan finance.

Is loan finance the right choice?

While loan finance can undoubtedly help your organisation achieve its objectives, it should, frankly, be the last resort after cheaper forms of finance, such as grants, sponsorship and fundraising. With most lenders, you'll be paying interest, possibly at a commercial rate. You'll be committed to repaying the capital sum. And you may need to offer security – which you could lose if something goes wrong and you're unable to pay back the interest and/or capital.

In looking at all the alternatives, there are other factors to bear in mind, over and above the need for the money itself. Although getting a loan will give you some financial credibility, it will not give you much else, whereas fundraising projects or extra contracts for services might raise your profile in the local community as a spin-off from raising more money.

Circumstances in which a loan might be appropriate include:

- taking out a mortgage to buy premises;
- providing bridging finance to overcome gaps in income until an expected grant arrives;
- borrowing to fund a new venture and using income from the venture's appeal to repay the loan, as the case study below shows.

CASE STUDY

An inner-city charity runs a women's refuge, and also provides support and rehabilitation facilities for victims of domestic violence. In response to growing demands for its services, it proposes to set up a second refuge and to take on an outreach worker to visit women in the community at large. At present it does not possess the £150,000 that the treasurer has calculated will be needed for the refuge and for the first few months' salary for a new member of staff. However, it does have a very committed band of supporters who can raise these funds over the next few years. The charity therefore plans to borrow £150,000 in the fairly certain knowledge that over the next five years it will be able to raise the money and interest through fundraising.

A word of warning – one very good reason *not* to borrow is that your organisation has simply run out of money altogether. In many scenarios specific measures can be taken to eliminate the resource gap. A situation in which your organisation is permanently scratching around for ways to plug the deficit is quite different. And while institutions which provide loans specifically to the voluntary sector are often willing to advance funds on less strict criteria than the commercial banks, even they are not going to lend if they feel that your organisation is in too precarious a situation to repay the funds.

It is also vital that your organisation thinks about where the repayment is going to come from. If you are just trusting to luck, then you shouldn't be thinking of loan finance at all. You would be much better off looking at other sources of funding or possibly joining forces with an organisation whose purposes are similar to yours.

Productive versus problematic borrowing

Borrowing can be considered to be the right funding option when it allows a voluntary organisation to do something positive, such as set up a scheme which would not otherwise be possible or start a project earlier than planned.

However, there is always a risk that things can go wrong, and if they do it can be expensive. There are three main reasons for this:

- The business plan was wildly optimistic, so the underlying assumptions on, say, future income turn out to be wrong.
- There is a change in the external climate which weakens the whole proposal, such as an unexpected withdrawal of funding or an increase in interest rates (this is very common). The case study below gives an example of this.
- There is mismanagement of the organisation or the project – either deliberate, or through foolhardiness, negligence or incompetence.

At any time, these events would probably bring in extra costs. But if a loan is involved, where repayments still have to be made from dwindling resources, or where an asset is called in by a lender, the result could be very great expense.

CASE STUDY

In 1989, the Central Young Men's Christian Association borrowed £31 million in order to buy back the leasehold interest in part of its premises in central London from The Housing Corporation so they could refurbish the premises and pay off certain liabilities. The intention was that when the property was refurbished, part of the premises would be sold or leased to a third party to be operated as a hotel. The proceeds would then be used to repay the loan. The loan was to be repaid within three years, as long as the property was disposed of within that period. The Governors of the Central YMCA obtained the consent of the Charity Commission.

In 1991, the property market turned sour and at the same time, the hotel business slumped as a result of the Gulf War and the IRA bombing in London. So the Governors of the Central YMCA were unable to repay the loan. They were forced to market the property to a limited number of potential purchasers, but the Charity Commission refused to give consent to the sale because the property had not been offered on the open market.

Three years later, however, the charity's financial position had improved and the part of the premises used as a hotel was sold on a long lease, allowing most of the debt to be paid off, but with the freehold of the whole site retained. The rest of the debt was expected to be repaid over the next eight years from the rent received from commercial lettings in the part of the building still owned by the charity. The large Club facilities were also retained and continue to be operated by the charity.

How much do you want to borrow?

There are two main elements to seeking finance – how much you want, and how long you want it for. Deciding how much you want to borrow should simply be a case of working out the total costs of the project or working capital, how much money is or will be available to pay for it (from, say, reserves, cash balances and any income coming in over the period during which the project is being set up) and subtracting one from the other. You should also put in a cushion for contingencies, such as extra costs which turn up unexpectedly when carrying out the project.

USING A CASH FLOW FORECAST

Of course, the sum is not that simple if you are dealing with revenue coming in, and expenditure going out, over a period of time. So you should construct a cash flow forecast for your organisation to see what the gap in resources really is. This should be fairly straightforward if you have a computer with standard business software.

The cash flow forecast is set out as a grid, with all your organisation's income and expenses listed vertically, and columns across the page for consecutive months. The examples given here are used by a charity providing support for people with a particular medical condition. Under the income heading would be included items such as those listed below:

Membership
Charity shop
Fundraising
Department of Health
Donations
Lottery grant
Other

Under the expenses heading you might include:

Salaries
Rent
Rates
Utilities
Telephone
Newsletter
Helpline
Charity shop

The difference between the total projected income and expenses will then give a surplus or deficit for each month. (Looking also at your profit and loss account will give you a wider picture as it includes accruals for income and expenditure which have not yet affected cash flow.) Any net surplus is then available to spend on the project being planned. If this is not sufficient to cover the project's costs, a loan might be appropriate. To calculate how much you would need to borrow, you should bring forward any net surplus or deficit, then work out cumulative totals to calculate what the worst financial position would be; this will then give you roughly the amount you are looking for.

CASE STUDY

A heritage centre in Lancashire wants to set up a permanent exhibition area with hand-operated looms and other historic machines, run by specially trained staff in eighteenth-century costume. This will produce handicrafts such as sweaters which can then be sold. There will be a small admission charge to the exhibition, with group discounts for schools, from which the centre hopes to get a lot of support.

The exhibition will cost £150,000 to create and equip with machinery, and £2,000 a month to run. The income from the exhibition after the first two months is calculated to be £3,000 a month (total income will be much higher in summer), so the net income for December will be £1,000.

The new exhibition will be set up in September and tested from October to November, when the centre is quiet. At present during this period, the centre usually makes a loss because most visitors come in summer. The exhibition will admit its first paying visitors in December and income will rise from then.

The cash flow forecast for the heritage centre, the net income/expenditure from the project, and the overall position are shown in the table on the following page (negative figures in brackets). There may be VAT and other tax considerations but, for simplicity, these have been ignored.

	Balance brought forward (cash in bank) £	Centre income/ expenditure £	Exhibition income/ expenditure £	Total income/ expenditure £
SEPT	30,000	2,000	(150,000)	(118,000)
OCT	(118,000)	1,000	(2,000)	(119,000)
NOV	(119,000)	(1,000)	(2,000)	(122,000)
DEC	(122,000)	–	1,000	(121,000)
JAN	(121,000)	1,000	2,000	(118,000)
FEB	(118,000)	2,000	3,000	(113,000)

So the heritage centre would need to borrow at least £122,000 and would need to show an improving financial position over subsequent months to cover repayments.

Most banks say that the amount they are prepared to lend is limited by the borrower's ability to service the debt, ie to make payments of interest and (where agreed) capital on the due dates. So you should also use your cash flow forecast to work out what your capacity will be to service the loan. (There is more information on borrowing limits in Chapter 6, see page 69.)

BUILDING IN A BUFFER

It is also vital to build in a buffer over and above what you think you'll need. If you borrow too little, you may run out of cash and have to ask for more money, which is hardly likely to go down well with the lender. This buffer is important for two reasons:

- in case you underestimate your own costs;
- in case interest rates go up and you are borrowing at a variable rate.

Changes in interest rate are important. The longer you borrow for the greater the risk that the financial climate will change. So do allow for your repayments to go up at some point.

On the other hand, don't overdo it – if you borrow much more than you need, you may end up taking on a burden you can't repay.

REPAYMENT PERIOD

Similarly, don't be too optimistic about how long you need the loan for. You may, for example, be expecting a grant to be paid within the next two months, so you take out a bridging loan for 60 days. If the grant is delayed – as is quite likely – you'll then have to go back to the lender and ask them to extend the term of the loan. It therefore makes sense to agree a term which is longer than you think you'll need. Then when you receive the grant, you can pay off the loan early. Ask your lender about a penalty-free early repayment arrangement.

EURO LOANS

Incidentally, though your loan will probably be offered in sterling, we are beginning to see loans also denominated in euros. These could mean you pay a very low rate of interest, but you'll be taking an exchange control risk unless the UK joins the single currency. So if you are considering a euro loan, you should proceed with considerable caution, although the risk would be less for organisations holding euro-denominated assets, which can be used to pay the loan back. You will not be exposed if the loan is to bridge an EU grant payable in euros.

Making a business plan

In order to apply for loan finance (including a bridging loan), you will have to make two business plans – one for your organisation generally, and one for the project being financed.

The plans should include the following:

- General information about your organisation, its history and objectives.

- Details of the 'market' in which your organisation operates and, if appropriate, a sales plan.
- The legal form your organisation has (eg registered charity) and proof that your organisation has the power to borrow.
- Details of assets owned and their value.
- Brief biographies of the key people managing your organisation.
- Finances:
  - A cash flow forecast (see page 40) for your organisation for at least the next 12 months (some lenders require it for two or three years). You should include the assumptions you have used in making the forecast; if there are large variations in income or expenditure between your forecast and your historic accounts, the lender will want to know why.
  - A current balance sheet.
  - Accounts for the past three years.
  - Latest management accounts.
  - Details of any borrowing history.

Once the business plan has been submitted as part of your loan application, don't think it has served its purpose. You should still be using it throughout the project as a route map to tell you where to go and how to get there. The lender will also need to see updated versions as the project progresses to give reassurance that the loan is being used as intended and that all is going according to schedule.

The decision to take out a loan

WHEN SHOULD IT BE DONE?

The answer is: well before you need the money. If your needs are straightforward, say for a bridging loan while you're waiting for a grant which can be fairly easily authenticated, then the process of getting a loan should be fairly swift. But if you are planning a project, with an uncertain outcome, then you should be talking to lenders as soon as possible. Even one or two years' notice would not be inappropriate.

HOW SHOULD IT BE DONE?

Steps to follow

The treasurer, or whoever controls your finances, should make the calculation of how much you need to borrow. (See 'Using a cash flow forecast', page 40.) If the funding is for a specific project, this calculation should be reviewed by whoever is running the project and endorsed by the governing body.

Your organisation will then start the hunt for a suitable lending arrangement. Once this has been agreed, the trustees (or directors) pass a formal resolution stating that they have agreed to borrow X amount from Y (lender), on the following terms (...), pledging the following assets (if any) as security and noting that relevant professional advice has been taken. It may be that they have to call a special meeting – the constitution should tell you this.

Checks and controls

It is important to ensure your organisation has proper checks and controls related to its borrowing activities.

Dealing with your bank – you should make sure your organisation has in place the right controls to stop unauthorised borrowing, particularly overdrafts (including simply going overdrawn on your current account). You need to have set out clearly in your agreement with your bank(s) how instructions will be given, who will authorise them (ie who will be the authorised signatories on the loan account), and what security checks will be used. It is best if all instructions are given to the bank in writing.

Checking your financial records – it goes without saying that the financial records of your organisation should be checked regularly to make sure that no unauthorised borrowing is taking place. This would include reviewing the bank statements to check for debit balances, and for unexpected sums of money paid into the account. If there are unexpected receipts, you should review the paperwork to find out why these amounts have been received, and ensure that they are not simply bank funds paid in by way of a loan. You also need to be alert to the possibility of money laundering, as offering a loan to a charity is one way of doing this. For more details see the companion guide on *Banking*, referred to below. In a trust, it will be the trustees' responsibility to oversee this process. As part of their job they should look at the management accounts at least monthly. In any organisation, you will also be conducting regular audits which should reveal any irregularities in your borrowing.

Segregation of duties – ideally, these checks should be built into a system of segregation of duties within your finance department. (Segregation of duties means that the person carrying out a task is different from the person recording it.) But if you, as treasurer, delegate the bookkeeping to someone else, you should carry out these checks yourself. If your organisation is so small that the finance function is carried out by one person, someone at a higher level such as a trustee or board member should carry out the checks.

There is more detail on financial checks in Chapter 9 of CAF's Money Management Guide, *Banking*.

CHAPTER 4

Where to go for loan finance

Loan finance has not always been an obvious option for voluntary organisations, but attitudes of lenders and circumstances of the organisations themselves are changing. This chapter provides a guide to the main types of lending institutions, to whom they will lend, in what situations and on what terms.

The lending scene

In the past, voluntary bodies have not been particularly attractive to commercial lenders – the specific reasons are outlined later in this chapter. Because of the dearth of conventional borrowing sources, therefore, some of the institutions operating in the social economy (ie organisations which give a high priority to social objectives) have developed schemes which are specially structured for voluntary organisations. And as these schemes grow in number, the financial credibility of voluntary organisations as a whole has slowly risen, with the result that mainstream lenders are gradually becoming more used to having them as borrowers. The fact that many voluntary organisations are now run like small businesses is also a factor in this gradual thaw.

With this change, however, has come the necessity for business-like practices to be followed in voluntary organisations so that lenders' requirements can be met.

If you are a voluntary organisation looking for loan finance, one of the main problems is that lending sources form a very fragmented market. While loans are available in the commercial sector, different banks will have different lending criteria, and levels of commitment to and understanding of voluntary organisations will vary. Some charitable trusts provide loan finance, but most do not. There are several banks with a social emphasis and lending intermediaries, but because of the different ways in which these structures operate, there is no central register of sources.

However, the following paragraphs should give some idea of what is available. As with anything else, you should also try to get names through your own voluntary sector contacts and networking groups. It may also be worth approaching organisations working with the small business sector, as small enterprises have a lot in common with voluntary organisations. (This also goes for business information generally – many trade associations and government bodies publish booklets covering the different aspects of running a small company, and listing services which are available. The Department of Trade and Industry produces a free guide to its publications aimed at small businesses, the *Small Business Publications Guide*, see Useful publications.)

Commercial banks and building societies

In the past, commercial banks have tended to shy away from lending to voluntary sector bodies. Many bank managers do not understand the financial impulse behind not-for-profit organisations, or the way in which their accounting works. They believe – often correctly – that many potential beneficiaries are unlikely to be able to service a loan because their income stream will not be sufficiently predictable, or simply not big enough, over the repayment period. This will be so especially where the borrowing is to provide working capital, rather than assets which can then be used as security for the loan. If security is provided, it may be difficult to sell if it is for a specialised use, such as a sports pavilion. And even if it can be sold, it may not be practicable to seize the assets if the borrower defaults – the banks have enough adverse publicity without risking press stories about them selling a charity's premises over its head!

However, most of them do say they can offer loan facilities to voluntary organisations in exactly the same way as they do to commercial enterprises. But you may find in practice that they are fairly cautious and rather more strict with the terms (see Chapter 2, page 29).

Some building societies lend on property, although mainly residential rather than commercial. The Nationwide, for instance, is a leading lender to housing associations. Several commercial banks regularly lend to the housing association sector, eg Nat West, Barclays and the Halifax.

Charitable trusts and foundations

Though established to give support to voluntary organisations primarily by way of grants, some charitable foundations now provide low-cost or interest-free loans as well. However, they do not like to advertise the fact, because, like the commercial banks, they are aware that borrowers in the voluntary sector are liable to have unpredictable income streams. Furthermore, since these trusts are already in the business of supporting the voluntary sector through grants, it is often easier for them to continue to donate money in this way, than via interest foregone on loans (effectively a donation) which would involve much more paperwork.

Where a charitable foundation is willing to provide loan finance, however, it is usually easiest in the first instance to offer it to organisations to whom grants have been given in the past, because there is an existing relationship. So if your organisation has been the beneficiary of grant funding, your first port of call could be to your donors to see if they are willing to offer you a loan.

Failing this, you can get *The Directory of Grant Making Trusts* and *Grantseeker* (a CD-ROM) from CAF and the *Guide to the Major Trusts* from the Directory of Social Change (see Useful publications). Though these trusts do not categorically state that loan finance is available, there may be a hint in the way an individual entry is written, such as 'From time to time, the XYZ Foundation has made a small amount of funding by way of loans'. If you do not have an existing relationship with a trust from which you are seeking a loan, approach them with an explanatory letter setting out the background to your organisation and the project or other reason for seeking a loan.

Lenders with a social emphasis

BORROWING VIA INTERMEDIARIES

A social investment intermediary is an organisation which channels money from lenders and investors – who may be institutions or individuals – to provide loan finance to voluntary organisations. Some funds may be directly brokered between the lender (say a commercial bank) and the borrower, others may be provided from a pool of funds raised from investors. The main purpose of these intermediaries is to help provide finance which would either not otherwise be available to the borrower, or not on terms tailored to the borrower's needs. There are now around a dozen investment intermediaries and most of the funds they provide come from the private and commercial sectors. A list of intermediaries and the sectors they service is included in the Appendix, and details of some of these are given below. More information on this subject can be found in *Social Investment and other financing techniques for voluntary organisations* by Malcolm Lynch (see Useful publications).

Aston Reinvestment Trust

Aston Reinvestment Trust provides loans at commercial rates to viable but not yet bankable projects in the voluntary and small business sector throughout Birmingham. The Trust operates as a mutual investment society and raises its money from organisations and individuals which are member investors.

Charities Aid Foundation/Investors in Society

Charities Aid Foundation (CAF) is itself a charity and offers a range of traditional banking and investment services for the voluntary sector as part of CAF Charity Services.

Additionally, CAF runs a social investment fund called Investors in Society. Money comes from both donations and interest-free deposits and is pooled to provide affordable loans and guarantees, mainly to borrowers with an annual income of between £100,000 and £1 million. There is currently a £100,000 maximum on loans. The loans often involve a partnership with other lenders such as commercial banks or charitable trusts. Interest is charged at a rate which is just enough to cover the administration costs while allowing the fund to be sustained.

CAF also operates a finance broking service which aims to match lenders and borrowers directly. CAF will consider lending to any not-for-profit organisations which exist to provide social or community benefit. There is no upper limit to the amount of the loan, and the interest rate is usually fixed.

CASE STUDY

The Hastings Trust helps to set up and support regeneration and development projects in Hastings, including environmental enhancement, and works through community groups with individuals, such as those who are unemployed.

The Trust was in rented accommodation and needed a permanent home which would save it rent, allow it to incorporate amenities such as disabled access, and earn extra income by setting up a resource centre which could be hired out for training.

However, every time the Trust found a suitable property, it was sold before funding could be negotiated. The Trust was not attractive to commercial lenders because it had no track record as a property developer, and no security to put in, as the value of the building after purchase and refurbishment was likely to be less than the costs involved. Furthermore, the Trust could not afford commercial rates of interest.

Having once again found a suitable building, the Trust approached Investors in Society. By now, the Trust had raised grants amounting to £90,000 from sources including English Partnerships and several private trusts, and after spending £55,000 to buy the property and £75,000 on refurbishment, a balance of £40,000 remained to be borrowed. Investors in Society agreed to lend the money, secured on charge, with interest charged at a fixed flat rate. They suggested that the Trust take out keyperson insurance in view of the key role played by the chief executive, which meant that if she was incapacitated or died, the loan would be repaid.

The Trust now occupies its own refurbished property, and it is in the process of buying the building next door.

Ecology Building Society

The Building Society lends money for the purchase of properties which, in the view of the Society, give an 'ecological payback'. This includes, for instance, derelict but sound houses which would otherwise have been abandoned, small-scale workshops, organic smallholdings and farms, and properties providing resources and facilities to promote the life of small communities. It will also consider lending on community premises, housing and charity shops.

The maximum amount lent is £275,000 and maximum loan to value is 80 per cent. The Building Society says it does not make a profit on valuation fees, keeps arrangement fees to a minimum, and does not charge a higher rate of interest for further advances.

Banks with a social emphasis

A couple of banks – Triodos and Unity Trust Bank – concentrate on project funding for the social economy.

Triodos is a social bank, and lends only to organisations and businesses whose objectives are of social and environmental value. The Bank is particularly interested in four main areas: charities (such as those providing special needs support and education), community projects (such as social housing), environmental initiatives (such as renewable energy) and social businesses including co-operatives and fair-trade businesses.

Loans are generally between £20,000 and £5 million and are usually provided for a term of between one and 20 years, or as a term mortgage for property purchase. Overdrafts, revolving credits and project finance are also available.

Unity Trust Bank is jointly owned by the trades union and co-operative movements, and was set up to provide low-cost banking services to clients in the social economy.

AFFINITY BANKING AND BORROWING

As has already been noted (see page 15), affinity borrowing involves a long-term, committed relationship between the voluntary organisation and the institution it is borrowing from. There are two main banks offering affinity banking and borrowing services.

Triodos Bank

Triodos Bank offers a range of savings accounts to individuals and charities including the Social Target Account. This enables depositors to target their savings to specific projects or loan sectors, for instance social housing or Third World development. Organisations borrowing from Triodos can explore with the Bank the possibility of encouraging supporters to open their own target accounts, which will allocate funds to the organisation's project. This helps reduce the loan interest rate.

An illustration of how a target account can be used is given in the case study below.

CASE STUDY

A Third World development charity needed to borrow £100,000 to fund a clean water project in Africa. Bank base rate was five per cent and a commercial loan was likely to cost the charity an extra margin on top of that.

The charity applied to a bank with a social emphasis, and took out a £100,000 loan. The bank ran a targeted account for savers who wanted to support overseas projects. Deposits in the account earned two per cent interest. The bank took a further two per cent to cover its costs, and was therefore able to lend the money to the charity at four per cent – one per cent below base rate.

NatWest Bank

NatWest Bank's Community Bond is designed to help local community groups which fall between grant funding and mainstream commercial finance. Savers invest in the bond for a fixed term, at a lower level of interest than the market rate. The Bank then donates the difference between the two rates to a regional charitable fund, which in turn lends the money to local community groups which are otherwise unable to access finance.

The regional community finance funds provide loans to charities and community groups in order to support economically viable enterprises which will significantly benefit a local community. Loan applications are adjudicated by a board which includes representatives both from the local community and from NatWest. There are no upper or lower limits for loans and interest is charged at or near commercial rates.

In addition to the service of these two banks, 'Partnership' accounts, such as the Just Housing Account launched in partnership with Churches National Housing Coalition, give savers another way to target funds to sectors they wish to support while earning competitive returns.

BORROWING FROM WITHIN THE COMMUNITY

Another option available to a voluntary organisation is to raise a loan with the help of its members and supporters, who can provide a guarantee to secure the borrowing. More details of this are given under Guarantee communities, (see page 16).

Through a 'Borrowing Community' scheme run by Triodos Bank it is possible for a group of supporters to make a loan to an organisation out of their own pockets. A group of supporters club together to take out a collective loan from Triodos which is handed over to the organisation. The supporters have to provide Triodos with repayment guarantees and other commitments but they then take on the loan repayments themselves, which are paid into a central account with the Bank. This is a useful way to prefinance fundraising – the supporters may otherwise have intended to covenant money to the organisation – but the loan means that the organisation gets the money immediately. More details of how borrowing communities operate are given on page 17.

CHAPTER 5

Choosing a lender

Having decided that a loan is what you need, and having seen the range of providers in the market, the next step is to make your choice. This chapter takes you through the process, explaining what you should look for, how to research your sources and how to approach a prospective lender.

How to find a lender

WHO SHOULD YOU APPROACH?

You should consider looking at more than one provider of loan finance, otherwise you can never be certain that your organisation is not paying over the odds for its loan. The voluntary sector has traditionally relied on personal contacts – a trustee or board member knowing someone who may be able to supply a loan – but it is always worth shopping around, perhaps looking at up to six alternatives. This is particularly important if your organisation is a charity, when the trustees have a legal obligation to get the best deal possible.

Your existing bankers

Normally your own clearing bank will be your first port of call. There can be several advantages in staying with your existing bankers:

- When it comes to loan finance the relationship with your lender could be just as important as the provision, and even the cost, of services. You have a track record with your existing bank and they may be more willing to be supportive, a factor which is especially important if things go wrong.

- For smaller loans – say, below £50,000 – the amount you save by going elsewhere is small in relation to the effort involved.
- It may be helpful from the point of view of your other banking needs not to sour the relationship by borrowing from another source. If you have financial problems a good relationship with your bank is more likely to result in your receiving their support through temporary difficulties.

Other providers

There are several good reasons for looking at a range of lenders, as well as that of getting the best deal for your organisation mentioned earlier:

- As we have seen in the previous chapter, there is now plenty of choice in the market. The attitude that an organisation unable to get a loan from their clearing bank would not be able to get one anywhere else no longer applies.
- If you are borrowing a substantial amount – say £1million or more – the cost of the loan can be more important than the relationship with your lender, making existing relationships less significant.
- Other banks may be interested in offering your organisation a loan and gaining an opportunity to bid for your day-to-day banking business.

RESEARCHING YOUR SOURCES

The relationship between your organisation and your lender can be more important than the nuts and bolts of the loan itself, as has already been mentioned. You should be looking for a lender with a commitment to the voluntary sector and who therefore understands the different kinds of pressures on voluntary organisations.

Specialist magazines for the voluntary sector, including *NGO Finance*, *Charity Times* and *Charity World* (see Useful addresses) publish annual banking surveys, which give an idea of the institutions you should approach. Banks which are actively seeking voluntary sector clients are likely to advertise in these publications – some of them have directory pages of professional services to the sector. Some lenders have charity units, or specialist units dealing with a particular type of customer, such as colleges of further education.

The monthly publication *Business Moneyfacts* contains a comprehensive listing of banks and building societies providing commercial mortgages, and bank business loans, and also indicates specific property sectors in which individual lenders are willing to advance money, such as care or nursing homes. For details of the cost of annual subscriptions or single copies, contact *Business Moneyfacts* direct (see Useful addresses). The listing includes contact phone numbers so you can ring up for the marketing literature.

HOW TO FIND INDEPENDENT ADVICE

You will need professional help in sorting out the financial aspects of the loan, and you should try to get advice from a firm of accountants or financial advisers with specialist experience of the voluntary sector. If this applies to your existing accountants, fine. If not, you should look in the regular listings and annual surveys produced by trade publications such as *NGO Finance* and *Charity Times*, which advertise the names of firms looking for business in the voluntary sector.

PROCEDURE FOR APPROACHING LENDERS

Bearing in mind all these considerations, what is the process you should go through to get those lending proposals on the table?

1 Once you have found the names of potential lenders, you should contact them by phone or letter to see what they are looking for in the way of information on your organisation, and tell them the reason you want to borrow. More details on this are given in Chapter 6.

2 You should then send them your business plan and other paperwork, following it up with a phone call to explain any information or calculations which may not be clear. It is quite likely that the lender will then want a meeting to go through your proposition, before going away to prepare a presentation. Remember that the lender may not be able to give you an immediate decision on your loan application, so you need to allow time for the approval process.

3 The next step is to prepare a shortlist of candidates and guidance on how to do this is given on page 66. If you are borrowing a larger amount, say over £500,000, you should arrange a formal 'beauty parade', preferably seeing presentations from all the contenders on the same day. Because of the time and trouble involved, however, this is not really necessary if you're borrowing smaller amounts. In this case it is probably sufficient to hold a less formal meeting or to make a decision on the basis of the information you already have.

What information does the lender need?

Different lenders of course have different requirements concerning the information they need when you apply for a loan. And very often, the process of applying for short-term bridging finance will be simpler than applying for funding for a longer-term project. However, the following list of requirements should act as the core of what you will be asked to provide. Try to produce a package which looks as professional as possible – this will help engender confidence on the part of the lender.

- Business plan (see Chapter 3, page 43)
  This will give the lender background information about your organisation as a whole. The other items below give information specifically about the project for which finance is being sought.
- Details of the basic proposal:
  - summary of the project and the needs it will meet;
  - why you need a loan and what you will use it for;

  - how much you need to borrow, whether you need the loan in one sum or in stages, when you need it to start, and for how long you need to borrow;
  - how much you, the borrower, can contribute and details of where this money will come from;
  - the security which is available, and whether any assets have already been used as security;
  - how you will repay the loan.
- The market:
  - details of the market or area in which the project will be active;
  - is there community support for the project and if so, what form does this take?
  - details of your market and, if appropriate, a sales plan.
- Legal background:
  - the legal form of the project, if this is set up as a separate operation;
  - details of how assets will be owned;
  - do you have all the necessary planning and other permissions?
- Key people:
  - brief biographies of the key people involved in the project;
  - details of the experience of any staff, if relevant.
- History:
  - a brief history of the development of the project.
- Finances:
  - a cash flow forecast for the project for at least the next twelve months. You should explain the assumptions you have made in producing the forecast. If there are large variations in income or expenditure between your forecast and your historic accounts, the lender will want to know why;
  - a budget for the project showing capital repayments and interest for three years or until the end of the loan, and forecast profit and loss accounts. It is a good idea to produce more than one budget for the project. The first should show the position if everything goes as planned, and

the second (or more) should allow for a worse performance, such as reduced income or higher interest rates, together with a note of how you could cut costs or raise additional income to compensate;
– a capital expenditure budget. This sets out the amount to be spent on assets of a lasting nature, such as buildings or equipment, rather than running costs such as heating;
– details of how much capital you already have, or have been promised;
– details of other existing or planned loans;
– a statement of how finances will be controlled, and by whom.

Information like this is vital to reassure the lender that you really do know how much money your organisation needs, and can monitor events once the loan has been made. Even if you cannot come up with the complete solution to your financial needs, the lender will want to know that you have at least gone through a rigorous logical process of finding out what those needs are, and what sort of help you are looking for.

How to interview the lender

The potential lenders will of course want to meet representatives from your organisation, both to clarify their understanding of the project being financed, and to see whether you are the kind of people they feel they can entrust their money to. There are several things you can do to give yourselves the best possible chance of success.

SUPPLY COMPLETE INFORMATION IN ADVANCE

Start off by giving the potential lender as much written information as possible in advance of the meeting, so that you don't waste their time (and yours) having to go through routine points once you get together. If there are any fundamental pieces of information which could make or mar your request for finance, do make sure you pick them up.

CASE STUDY

A theological college wanted to set up a sister organisation in Africa, and applied to its bank for a loan to give it start-up working capital. The bursar knew that the bank would probably want to place a mortgage on the college buildings, and began to look for the title deeds, but became distracted by the task of preparing the year-end accounts. He knew the buildings were unlikely to be owned by anyone else, so he sent the bank the requisite paperwork, and arranged a meeting.

The day before the meeting, the bishop of the local diocese popped into the college for a chat, and started reminiscing about the college's early days. To the bursar's horror, he made a reference to the Church's ownership of the buildings. The bursar checked with the Church authorities and found that they did indeed own the property.

At the meeting the next day, the bank manager raised the question of security for the loan, and the bursar had to confess that the college buildings were not available. This got things off on the wrong foot, as the bank manager had assumed that they would be. It also made the bursar look ill-informed. The college did not get the loan from the bank.

WHO SHOULD ATTEND?

At the meeting with a potential lender, your organisation will no doubt be represented by whoever has the day-to-day responsibility for the loan, ie your chief executive and/or whoever is in charge of the finances. However, it's also useful for one of your trustees or board members to come along as well, to put up a united front and show that you have support from the highest level of the organisation. (Incidentally, many lenders have a rather jaundiced view of the board of trustees or directors – they may feel they are very passive, and do things out of the goodness of their hearts, but do not understand their liabilities and obligations. So it is important for individuals at this level to show that they are sufficiently informed on the issues involved in the loan to act as an effective check, even if they are not involved in it on a day-to-day basis.)

As with any other interview, first impressions count, and the lender's representatives are likely to get a gut feel when they meet you. So you should convey enthusiasm and commitment towards the cause for which you are borrowing the money, and show you have a clear vision of the outcome.

KNOW YOUR SUBJECT

Where you are looking to borrow for a specific project, make sure you have a very good grasp of the economics of the project to reassure lenders that the figures they have been supplied with are valid, and that you know what's going on. Make sure you can show them the process you went through in planning the project, including tests such as carrying out a feasibility study, so that it's obvious you have built up a strong case for it, rather than its simply being the whim of the chief executive.

This is also important so you can keep the meeting as brief as possible; time is money for the bank staff, and they are unlikely to be impressed if you start flannelling because you don't have the facts at your fingertips!

KNOW HOW YOUR LENDER OPERATES

At an early stage in the process, you should find out what tests each bank uses, and in what order, to assess loan applications. Do they first assess your business plan, and then secondly how you plan to repay the loan, or do they first look at the security you can offer, and then your business plan? Some banks may demand the kind of security which your organisation cannot offer (see Chapter 1). Ruling out at an early stage criteria you cannot meet will save time later on.

CONVEY YOUR PROFESSIONALISM

On a more general level, you have to persuade them that your organisation is very professionally managed, and could therefore run the project efficiently and effectively. With smaller voluntary organisations in particular, banks and building societies may be on the look-out for signs that your organisation is run by 'do-gooders' with little professional experience. So you should know where the organisation is going and what its mission and objectives are, although this should also be included in your business plan. You should aim to show that you have a tight grip on your organisation's finances, and that there are sufficient checks and balances in the system to allow proper control over the project (see page 45), and to alert you well before things go wrong. This also means allocating responsibilities to individual people – again, a lender's nightmare is for things to go wrong, with individuals shuffling responsibility on to each other, instead of taking the initiative to sort things out.

BE HONEST!

Do be honest about any financial difficulties your organisation has had in the past. The lenders may well find out about them later. But in fact, showing that you have survived problems in the past can work to your advantage.

You should also at this stage make the lender aware of any circumstances which may affect your ability to service the loan in a straightforward manner. This is a key requirement for borrowers. If, for instance, you cannot start to make repayments immediately, the lender may give you a period of grace on capital repayments. However, lenders like their interest to be repaid on time, if only because of the fact that the borrower is technically in default if it is not.

CASE STUDY

A charity which ran a small group of almshouses decided to refurbish them and applied for a loan to its bank. The refurbishment was expected to take three or four months, during which time the tenants would have to be rehoused, and the charity would therefore forego its rental income. This meant that the charity was not going to be able to meet the repayments on the loan during the period of refurbishment.

The bank suggested that the charity either held back some cash from its normal outgoings to cover the interest payments, or borrowed more money than was actually needed to carry out the refurbishment in order to meet the repayments.

If a borrower does foresee difficulties in paying the interest over a defined period, the lender often suggests increasing the loan to enable them to do that.

LINKS WITH OTHER ORGANISATIONS

It is also a good idea to tell potential lenders about any support you are likely to get from a sponsoring organisation, such as the Church, or an umbrella organisation, if things go wrong. And if you are working in an area which is regulated, such as the housing association sector – which is monitored by The Housing Corporation – you should point this out to the lenders. Again, this will indicate that you are likely to follow best practice in the way your organisation manages its affairs.

SUCCESSION

In addition, the lender may want to discuss the question of succession: if the project, or in fact your organisation, is largely driven by a dynamic individual, what happens if they fall under the proverbial bus? One solution would be for you, the borrowers, to take out keyman insurance and assign the proceeds to the lender. Sometimes this may be a condition of getting the loan. However, you should also have a contingency plan worked out in terms of who would take over the running of the project if the worst happens.

Drawing up a shortlist

Having contacted several institutions, you will then want to whittle them down to a shortlist of two or three.

WHO TO ELIMINATE

From your preliminary dealings with these lenders, the candidates for elimination will be fairly obvious. These will be lenders who:

- send you a quote with costs which are substantially out of line with the others;
- demand security which you do not have;
- do not show much enthusiasm in replying to your enquiry, or take a long time to reply.

LOCATION OF THE LENDERS

At this stage, you should also consider the relative proximity of the lenders in question. This is more of an issue if you are looking at commercial lenders (such as clearing banks) because there is likely to be more choice of location. You're obviously not going to be in frequent contact with your lender, but there may be times when you do want personal contact.

If the branch closest to you were to be shut down, where would the nearest one be? A loan cannot be moved in the same way as a cheque account. Moving your loan arrangements to another branch of the same bank means you will probably be dealing with a new set of people who may not be as flexible as those at your previous branch. They may have different criteria if you wish to amend some of the terms. You may be especially vulnerable with a bank whose natural sphere of operations is not where you are based, such as a Scottish bank in England, and vice versa. In this situation, the bank's network may be sketchy and if there are closures, the nearest branch could be a long way away.

IMPLICATIONS FOR YOUR OTHER BANKING

Some lenders now insist that borrowers move their current account to them as well. This is not necessarily as self-interested as it may seem: the person at the bank who agrees to lend to you is making themselves vulnerable to the risk that your organisation will not be able to repay the loan, and they may feel they should put themselves in a position to monitor your cash flow in case things go wrong. If switching your bank account is part of the deal, you'll obviously have to include your satisfaction (or otherwise) with your present bankers as a factor in your decision. And the question of location will also then relate to your day-to-day current account activities.

YOUR RELATIONSHIP WITH THE LENDER

Once you've taken out the loan, your lender might move its local branch manager. In this case it will help if you've already established a relationship with other staff at the branch – again a good reason to place a high priority on the quality of the relationship you develop when you're choosing a lender.

The size of your loan, however, will determine the level of seniority at which it is dealt with inside the bank – locally, regionally or at head office. Especially with a clearing bank, the further up the line you go, the more the bank's response will depend on what you present to them in terms of factual information. At these higher levels, you may find that a good relationship with the banking staff you deal with on a day-to-day basis is irrelevant when setting the parameters for the loan.

There are other 'spin-off' factors which are of lesser importance in making your choice of lender, but which may influence you if there is little difference between what the lenders are offering. These include the opportunity to make contact with other voluntary sector groups through a bank's charity services, and opportunities for joint activities with the lender which could promote your cause.

CHECKLIST FOR CHOOSING A LENDER

- Research possible sources of funding.
- Contact the most suitable, and find out what information they need in order to consider your application.
- Submit your proposal, together with the appropriate back-up documentation.
- Sift through the responses and draw up a shortlist.
- Invite the shortlisted lenders to make presentations.
- Decide between the final candidates, if necessary having further conversations or meetings to negotiate better terms.

CHAPTER 6

Negotiating a loan

Once you have arrived at a shortlist of lenders, you will be getting down to the detail of negotiating the precise terms of your loan. This chapter explains one of the key elements in this process – the cost of the loan – and advises you on how to make your final decision, bearing in mind the other key element – your relationship with your lender. Finally, some pointers are given on the formal requirements involved in the signing and sealing process.

How much will you pay?

HOW TO DECIDE ON YOUR BORROWING LIMIT

Your borrowing limit is not the same as the amount you think you *need* to borrow: it is the maximum amount that you are likely to be *able* to borrow from the lender.

There are three main aspects to working out this figure:

1 How much do you need to borrow to be able to complete the purchase or to see the project through? In your business plan and cash flow forecast you will have to calculate the minimum requirement based upon the funds you have available and known or foreseeable costs (see page 39). You should always build in some sort of contingency to cushion you against overruns or unexpected expenses.

2 How much can you realistically borrow against the strength of your organisation's balance sheet and/or the available security? Lenders will each have their own internal guidelines, but they are likely to restrict unsecured lending to an amount no bigger than the net worth (ie total assets less total

liabilities) of your organisation. Larger facilities will generally need to be secured, and you can expect a commercial lender to advance in the region of 70 per cent of the value of a property taken as security. (Banks operating with a social emphasis and similar lenders may have more flexible limits.) A lower percentage advance may apply if the building is of a specialised nature, has restrictive covenants or inflexible planning consent.

3 How much can you afford to repay, and can your ability to repay be demonstrated? Ideally, you should be able to show what your repayment ability is from your organisation's historical surpluses and cash flows after allowing for any new costs. A lender will be concerned if they think you are relying too much on grant funding, particularly if a long-term loan is required and the grant funding is agreed on an annual basis. If the new project is to generate the funds to repay the loan, or is to bring about cost savings that will cover the repayments, you will have to be able to show convincingly the additional income or cost savings. In all these calculations, the lender will want you to build in a margin for error.

Having now arrived at your three borrowing figures, the amount you will be able to borrow is the lowest of the three. However, if the first figure (ie how much money you need) is not the lowest, then you will have problems in raising the finance. If the lowest figure is the third (the amount you can afford to repay) then the project is not viable as it stands.

HOW TO WORK OUT THE COST OF A LOAN

You can get a rough idea of what your loan repayments will be by using one of two different methods. Suppose an organisation borrows £10,000 at ten per cent over five years:

- If the whole amount is repaid at the end of the period, you can work out the repayments as follows:

  The interest is £10,000 x 10% x 5 = £5,000.

  So, the monthly repayments are £5,000 divided by 60 = £83.33 per month, plus a final payment of £10,000.

- If the capital is paid off with the interest, the interest is calculated on the average balance outstanding at regular intervals, say each month. You will need tables to work out the amounts of the repayments, otherwise you will have to ask the lender for a schedule (see below).

To confirm these calculations, early on in your negotiations you should ask the lender for a repayment schedule. This should be broken down between capital and interest and it should tell you what the interest rate is, and how the rate varies (if at all) in comparison with base rate.

Fixed and variable interest rates

As with personal borrowing such as a mortgage, the interest rate on your organisation's loan will normally be linked to the prevailing rate of interest, ie it is variable. The lender will always seek a buffer to cover its own costs and the unexpected, and so interest will be charged at a margin above either base rate or Libor (London Inter-Bank Offered Rate). The latter is the rate at which banks will lend in the inter-bank market, and it is a benchmark for wholesale interest rates. The Libor rate tends to anticipate future interest rate trends – if the market thinks interest rates will rise, the Libor rate is normally higher than base rate, and vice versa.

The margin usually varies and depends on several factors:

- who the lender is, and their own costing structure;
- the perceived risk to the lender – the riskier the project or borrower, the higher the margin;
- the size of the loan – the margin may decrease the larger the amount borrowed;
- whether there is security – if so, the margin will be less;
- there may be accepted norms for the sector in which your organisation operates, such as for nursing homes.

With larger loans, the interest rate margin may vary over time. For instance, it might start off at 0.75 per cent over base and then be cut to 0.5 per cent after two years, when the project being financed is well advanced and the lender considers the risk to their money has diminished. As an alternative, you may be able to fix the rate of interest you are charged by the lender. This is quite a common arrangement for money loaned above a certain amount, for instance £100,000. The advantage is that your interest payments will be fixed, allowing you to budget more easily. However, you will normally only be able to fix the rate for an agreed period, typically five years. After this length of time, the interest rate you pay will vary in line with market rates.

If you are in a position to make a choice between a fixed rate and a variable rate loan, you decide which to go for using the same criteria as for a fixed rate or variable mortgage. If you think interest rates will fall, you are likely to choose a variable rate. But if you are wrong and rates go up, you will have to pay more interest. A fixed rate is better if you think rates will rise in the future.

Rather than take out a fixed rate loan, you can protect against interest rate fluctuations by taking a 'cap and collar' loan for which a premium may be charged. This is a variable rate loan with an upper and lower limit on the interest rate charged, so if rates generally rise above the limit, you will carry on paying interest at that level, and vice versa if rates fall below the lower limit.

Negotiating interest rates

If you feel you are on fairly firm ground and are likely to get offers from several lenders, you may feel you are in a position to negotiate a lower interest rate. You should, however, be aware that it is considered unethical to show or disclose the rates that other lenders have given you in order to bargain them down. However, what you can do is to indicate that you'd like to do business with someone, but that they need to be a bit more competitive. But you should realise that potential lenders with whom you have no existing relationship will not be too pleased if it becomes obvious that you are using them as a means of driving home a bargain with your existing clearing bank. You never know when you will be forced to go shopping again for financial services, and you don't want to queer your pitch with future providers!

The borrowing period

It is important to bear in mind the real cost of borrowing when you are considering the period of your loan. For instance, a loan over twenty-five years can cost far more than a 10-year loan at a higher rate of interest.

Additional charges

As well as the interest charged on the loan, you may be expected to pay any of the following:

- Arrangement fees paid to the lender for setting up the facility. These will be between 0.5 per cent and one per cent of the value of the loan, and will be paid upfront.
- Extra fees paid to the lender depending on how the money is taken – for instance, if you are drawing instalments of the loan over a long period, you may have to pay a fee on the amounts you haven't yet drawn.
- If the lender wants security, this will involve legal costs. You may also have to pay for valuations.
- If the loan is taken out to convert a property, the lender may wish to receive regular architect's reports on the progress of the conversion.
- Early repayment penalties.

METHODS OF REPAYING

The three main ways of repaying the capital are (see also pages 12–13):

- monthly repayments;
- one or more lump sum payments throughout the term of the loan;
- a 'bullet' repayment at the end of the term. This is not popular with lenders for long-term loans.

You may be able to get the lender to agree to some flexibility in repaying the capital.

CASE STUDY

A charitable trust running a special needs centre from an old Victorian house planned to move to a purpose-built centre, which would be paid for from an appeal and from increased revenue as the trust expanded its activities. The loan was to be disbursed in stages as the building work was carried out, but the increased income would not start to flow until the building was completed – about six months after the start of the project. So the lender agreed to defer the capital repayments for the first six months until the increased fees from local authorities started to come in.

Another way for a lender to give some leeway is to ask for low capital repayments to begin with, building them up as time goes on.

The golden rule in planning loan repayments is to match the repayment schedule with the income streams coming into your organisation. But however you repay the capital, you are likely to have to make interest repayments from day one.

Unexpected costs

Over and above the borrowing costs which you can predict, there may be other extras that you hadn't bargained for. Some of the things to look out for are listed below, but it is always worth making sure you have built in a buffer (see page 42) to deal with these contingencies.

- If you do not pay interest on time, the lender may not call in the loan, even if you are in default. The lender will advise you what course of action is to be taken. One option would be to start rolling up the interest as capital. In this case, you start paying interest on interest within a month.

- If interest is to be rolled up, at what point is the unpaid interest capitalised, ie added to the debt? This is important because once it has been capitalised, you will start paying interest on the interest, sometimes referred to as default interest. Some lenders do this monthly, some annually, others never.
- Bear in mind the terms on which a variable interest rate may be amended. If it is amended only once a year, then if interest rates are going down, you're not going to get the benefit for up to a year (though, conversely, you'll get a period of adjustment if interest rates are going up).
- If the loan is made as a facility which you then draw down as you need funds, you may be charged for the funds you don't use. It is fairly common, particularly for large loans, for banks to charge a 'non-utilisation' fee on the unused money, as compensation to them for the fact that they can't be using that money elsewhere.
- If you are using an older property as security for the loan, the title may be unregistered and you may have to pay to register title. Check your title to any property you're thinking of using as security, and if it doesn't exist, budget for the extra costs. You could expect to pay anything up to £2,000. It is possible to insure against unregistered or unclear title: your current insurers or a broker could advise you.
- If a charity has occupied a property for a long time, it may be that the title deeds have been lost. This will mean additional costs for carrying out a Land Registry search (if the property is registered) and getting a duplicate title deed, or getting an affidavit signed by two trustees or directors stating that the property is owned by your organisation.

Making the final decision

At the end of the day, you will be choosing both the lender and the financial package on offer as a combined entity. There are two main issues to consider – cost and your relationship with the lender.

You should, generally speaking, go for the cheapest. That is easier said than done, because the interest rate (or interest margin, because most loans tend to be at variable rates set at base rate plus a certain percentage) may vary over time. Remember to include the extra costs such as arrangement fees.

However, you should also consider which lender – both as an institution and in terms of the people you're dealing with – you think you'd get on with best. You may get some guidance on this from whether or not they have experience of the voluntary sector, or even better, a dedicated voluntary sector unit. In addition, it is obviously important to have a rapport with the staff with whom you'd be dealing once you agree the loan.

Flexibility is crucial, and if someone has shown flexibility in the negotiation process, then that suggests they will be prepared to give you leeway further down the line. And of course, there is always the possibility that things could go wrong, in which case you certainly will need to feel that you're dealing with someone who is prepared to be reasonable. So even if you've got the cheapest deal, you should think twice before you enter into a relationship with someone you're not keen on.

This is probably a more important factor than the price of the loan, as long as the lender is not massively out of kilter with its competitors.

The lender's formal requirements

Once you have agreed terms, the lender will want to see certain documents before you sign the formal agreement. The lender needs to be convinced that your organisation is able to manage the money and the project properly.

DOCUMENTATION

This includes:

- Your organisation's governing document, such as its trust deed (for a charitable trust) or, for an incorporated company, its Memorandum and Articles of Association, along with its certificate of incorporation confirming it is a properly registered company.
- Proof that your organisation is empowered to borrow, and has the power to charge its assets, if the lending is secured. The lender may also want to know what the trustees' or directors' powers are – for instance, what they can commit the organisation to without, say, calling an extraordinary meeting. These powers may be contained in the governing document. If not, there may be implied powers given by law (see Chapter 2). However, most lenders are likely to insist that the powers are expressly stated in the governing document.
- A certified copy of the resolution to borrow, passed by your trustees or directors. This should contain evidence that the trustees or directors have accepted the terms and agreed to sign the loan offer together with any security documents.
- If you're a charity registered in England or Wales and you are mortgaging property, the lender will want to see a copy of the written advice you have received from someone with professional expertise. See Section 38(2) of the Charities Act 1993.
- The lender may also want to verify the costs involved with the project being financed. For instance, if you're converting a property, you might be asked to provide a surveyor's report giving a breakdown of the refurbishment costs involved. Similarly, you should include proof that you have complied with regulatory requirements, such as a copy of any necessary planning permission from the local council.
- If you're seeking bridging finance to tide you over until you receive a grant, the lender will probably want to see proof that the grant will be paid, such as a letter from the organisation making the grant.
- The business plan for the project being financed.

PROOF OF YOUR COMPETENCE TO MANAGE THE MONEY

Most lenders would probably say that when an organisation comes to them for a loan, the three most important factors in deciding whether to say 'yes' are management, management and management – of the borrower, that is. So the lender will want to know how your organisation has been managed, who the management are and what their track record is (see 'What information does the lender need', page 59). Lenders are likely to make credit checks on the key people, as well as on the organisation itself, and get bank references. In addition to the biographical details of key people, it will be helpful if you give them a CV for your organisation plus a couple of references – for instance, individuals at other organisations with whom you have a funding or operational relationship.

PROOF OF YOUR COMPETENCE TO MANAGE THE RELATED PROJECT

Again, the lender will want to see that your organisation possesses the balance of skills normally associated with running a business. So they will want similar reassurance to that described above, but in the context of the actual project being financed.

What happens next?

This all depends on the individual lender, but typically, an outline offer will be made, called the heads of terms. This deals with the basic terms of the facilities such as:

- how much will be lent;
- for how long the money will be lent;
- what interest will be charged;
- what other costs will be charged;
- what security is required;
- what documentation is needed;

- what ongoing monitoring the lender will need to carry out once the loan is made.

If the terms are acceptable, you sign and return the form, and the lender will then produce formal documentation.

Even then, the lender will continue to carry out due diligence checks. For instance, if there is a property involved, the lender will want to look at it to check it exists and to confirm its value. Similarly, where a building is to be used to provide services, the lender will also want to assess whether it is appropriately located and can be converted as required.

CHAPTER 7

Evaluating your loan

As well as describing steps you can take to keep your borrowing running smoothly, this chapter offers advice on how to assess whether the right decision has been made and what to do if things go wrong along the way.

Avoiding difficulties

On the basis that prevention is better than a cure, take care that your in-house administration is properly organised. Once the loan agreement is in place, you should make sure that you comply with all the covenants, such as providing management information every quarter, or taking out insurance on the property used as security or keyman insurance on the individual driving the project. The lender may well remind you about these, but you should still put a diary note in place so you remember when insurance premiums, or whatever, are due.

Also, ensure your administrative systems provide adequate checks and controls on your borrowing activities (see page 45).

Have you made the right decision?

The short answer is, you'll probably only know if you've made the wrong decision! There are warning signals which can tell you that things are not going as planned.

- Interest rates may have risen substantially over the term of the loan, and you are struggling to make repayments. You might have been better off fixing the rate.
- You are unable to live with the undertakings to comply with the covenants in the loan agreement. This really emphasises

how important it is to take a detailed look at the agreement before you sign it, and to get specialist advice.

There may, however, be problems not with the loan itself, but with the purpose it was meant to help carry out – for instance, the project may not have given rise to the income you expected. In this case, you'll have paid out both the cost of the project and loan interest for a negative outcome.

When to renegotiate terms

You may feel it necessary to renegotiate the terms of your loan if:

- you are having problems making your repayments;
- you want to pay off the loan early;
- you need more money than you originally envisaged;
- you find the covenants in the loan agreement difficult to comply with.

Trying to change the terms of an agreement can, however, leave a bad taste in the lender's mouth – in most cases lenders are reluctant to do it. If they do agree, they may demand some recompense, such as a higher margin of interest. As with all the other aspects of borrowing, the best protection is to get a solicitor to read the agreement before you sign it. And you should try to get flexibility written into the terms at the outset.

Should you extend the loan?

You may want to extend the loan if your organisation cannot meet the repayment programme, either in terms of the regular repayments of capital or the bullet repayment at the end of the term. Most lenders will agree to look at extending the facility if they consider there is a good reason for it. However, they are quite likely to build a premium into the new arrangement, either by charging a higher interest rate or a one-off fee. Again, this underlines how important it is to do your sums properly before you agree the loan in the first place, as the lender is then in the driving seat.

Dealing with default

A default can either take the form of inability to make payments, or more technical shortcomings such as failing to meet a covenant, like supplying information. Once a default is triggered, the lender has the right to demand full payment of the amount which has been lent. Alternatively, the lender (or any other creditor) with a charge on any of the organisation's assets can apply to have a receiver appointed if they think there is a threat to the asset given as security (see page 33), or if the loan is unlikely to be repaid.

Defaulting on a loan is a problem, but lenders do have a number of options at their disposal with which to remedy the situation. It may not be in the lenders' interests to pull the rug from under a borrower's feet, and they may therefore want to agree a rescue plan. They may, for instance, agree to extend the term of the loan and reduce the monthly repayments. Or they may agree to forego capital repayments for a period, and convert the loan to one operating on an interest-only basis. If your organisation has a repayment mortgage, and has already paid off some capital, this will be taken into consideration too.

However, it is important to realise that the lender's reaction will depend partly on who brings the default to their notice. If you realise that your organisation has problems with repayments and tell the lender immediately, you're giving yourselves the best chance of a sympathetic hearing. If it is the lender, however, who discovers the default, then they are likely to take a more serious attitude.

The lender has to decide whether to remedy the situation or take pre-emptive action. If the default has obviously been remedied, then the lender will not want to precipitate matters by calling in the loan and possibly losing their money. If they do take action, they may send in an independent firm of accountants to look at the situation, a course of action for which you will be billed.

Problems with your lender

A loan arrangement can be vulnerable to the same sort of mistakes as your normal current account with a bank. Sometimes interest is wrongly calculated, or payments are not credited. More seriously, you may realise that the terms of the loan were not made clear to you when you set up the arrangement.

If the lending staff you are in contact with are unable to sort out the problem to your satisfaction, you should use the lender's own complaints procedure to resolve the situation.

THE BANKING OMBUDSMAN SCHEME

If, having exhausted your lender's complaints' procedure, you are still dissatisfied, you can take your complaint to the Banking Ombudsman (see Useful addresses), as long as your lender is a member. Practically all the UK's commercial banks are members of the scheme, but most banks with a social emphasis and loan companies are not.

The Banking Ombudsman scheme can be used by unincorporated associations such as charities and clubs, and also by limited companies with an annual turnover below £1 million (but only for events which took place on or after 26 January 1993). The scheme cannot be used where the complaint:

- relates to any commercial judgements unless there has been maladministration or inequitable treatment;
- relates to an event which occurred more than six years ago (unless you could not reasonably have known about it until after then);
- is being, or has been, dealt with by a court, unless the bank gives written agreement for it to be investigated by the Ombudsman;
- relates to a claim for over £100,000;
- relates to a banking service provided outside the UK.

Once the Ombudsman has checked that he can deal with the complaint, a totally independent investigation is undertaken. If the bank is a member of the scheme, it must accept his recommendations. But even if the decision goes against you, you still have the right to take legal action.

There is a separate Building Societies Ombudsman scheme (see Useful addresses) which works in a similar way, and can be used by organisations with an annual turnover of under £1 million.

Appendix

SOCIAL INVESTMENT INTERMEDIARIES*

Intermediary	Type of activity supported
Aston Reinvestment Trust	Charities, community enterprise, small business
Co-operative Finance Housing Society	Housing co-operatives
Ecology Building Society	Property-related loans
Employee Ownership Loan Fund Scotland	Worker co-operatives, employee buy-outs
Glasgow Regeneration Fund	Community enterprise, small business
The Housing Finance Corporation	Housing associations
Industrial Common Ownership Finance	Worker co-operatives, community enterprise
Investors in Society (CAF)	Charities and not-for-profit organisations
Local Investment Fund	Development trusts, community enterprise
NatWest Community Bond	Community enterprise
Radical Routes	Housing co-operatives
Shared Interest Society	Third World community business development
Triodos Bank	All social economy organisations including charities

* **Source** *Social Investment and other financing techniques for voluntary organisations* by Malcolm Lynch (see Useful publications)

Useful addresses

Business Moneyfacts
Moneyfacts House
66-70 Thorpe Road
Norwich
Norfolk NR1 1BJ
Tel 01603 476100

There is also a Faxback service for commercial mortgages: *Tel* 090 607 607 06. Calls cost a maximum of 75p per minute. For problems in transmission there is a helpline on 01603 476500.

Charity Commission
Harmsworth House
13-15 Bouverie Street
London EC4Y 8DP
Tel 0870-333 0123

Charity Commission
2nd Floor
20 King's Parade
Queen's Dock
Liverpool L3 4DQ
Tel 0870-333 0123

Charity Commission
Woodfield House
Tangier
Taunton
Somerset TA1 4BL
Tel 0870-333 0123

Charity Times
408 The Fruit & Wool Exchange
Brushfield Street
London E1 6EP
Tel 020 7426 0424

Charity World
70 Queen's Head Street
London N1 8NG
Tel 020 7359 1934

Directory of Social Change
24 Stephenson Way
London NW1 2DP
Tel 020 7209 5151
Fax orders 020 7209 5049

Factors & Discounters Association
Boston House
The Little Green
Richmond
Surrey TW9 1QE
Tel 020 8332 9955
Web site www.factors.org.uk

Finance & Leasing Association
4th Floor
Imperial House
15–19 Kingsway
London WC2B 6UN
Tel 020 7836 6511

Financial Intermediaries and Claims Office (FICO)
Charity Technical Unit
St John's House
Merton Road
Bootle
Merseyside L69 9BB
Tel 0151-472 6046

Financial Services Authority
Public Enquiries Office
25 The North Colonnade
Canary Wharf
London E14 5HS
Tel 0845-606 1234

NGO Finance
3 Rectory Grove
London SW4 0DX
Tel 020 7819 1200

The Office of the Banking Ombudsman
70 Gray's Inn Road
London WC1X 8NB
Tel 020 7404 9944
Lo-call 0345 660902

The Office of the Building Societies Ombudsman
Millbank Tower
Millbank
London SW1P 4XS
Tel 020 7931 0044

The Stationery Office
For information about publications and orders:
Tel 0870-600 5522
Web site www.tsonline.co.uk
E-mail books.orders@theso.co.uk
Fax 0870-600 5533

Useful publications

Banking Act 1987 Exempt Transactions Regulations 1997 (Statutory Instrument 817), price £6.50, available from the Stationery Office (see Useful addresses)

Charities Act 1993, price £4.30, available from the Stationery Office (see Useful addresses)

The Directory of Grant Making Trusts 1999–2000 16th edition, published by CAF, price £89.95 (3 volumes)

Grantseeker – The interactive CD-ROM for fundraisers, produced by CAF, price £58.69 for each six-monthly release

Guide to the Major Trusts, 2 volumes, price £19.95 and £18.95. Available from the Directory of Social Change (see Useful addresses), post and packing £2.50

Small Business Publications Guide, reference number 99/814, produced by the Department of Trade and Industry, available free, tel 0870 1502 500

Social Investment and other financing techniques for voluntary organisations by Malcolm Lynch, published by CAF, price £14.95

CHARITY COMMISSION BOOKLETS

(available from Charity Commission offices, see Useful addresses)

CC3 *Responsibilities of Charity Trustees*

CC3(a) *Responsibilities of Trustees: A Summary*

CC33 *Acquiring Land*

A Guide to the Charities Acts 1992 & 1993

About CAF

CAF, Charities Aid Foundation, is a registered charity with a unique mission – to increase the substance of charity in the UK and overseas. It provides services that are both charitable and financial which help donors make the most of their giving and charities make the most of their resources.

Many of CAF's publications reflect the organisation's purpose: *Dimensions of the Voluntary Sector* offers the definitive financial overview of the UK voluntary sector, while *The Directory of Grant Making Trusts* provides the most comprehensive source of funding information available.

As an integral part of its activities, CAF works to raise standards of management in voluntary organisations. This includes the making of grants by its own Grants Council, sponsorship of the Charity Annual Report and Accounts Awards, seminars, training courses and the Charities Annual Conference, the largest regular gathering of key people from within the voluntary sector. In addition, Charitynet (www.charitynet.org) is now established as the leading Internet site on voluntary action.

For decades, CAF has led the way in developing tax-effective services to donors, and these are now used by more than 250,000 individuals and 2,000 of the UK's leading companies, between them giving £150 million each year to charity. Many are also using CAF's CharityCard, the world's first debit card designed exclusively for charitable giving. CAF's unique range of investment and administration services for charities includes the CafCash High Interest Cheque Account, two common investment funds for longer-term investment and a full appeals and subscription management service.

CAF's activities are not limited to the UK, however. Increasingly, CAF is looking to apply the same principles and develop similar services internationally, in its drive to increase the substance of charity across the world. CAF has offices and sister organisations in the United States, Bulgaria, South Africa, Russia, India and Brussels.

For more information about CAF, please visit www.CAFonline.org

Other publications from CAF

A series of one-stop guides on a variety of core activities, the titles appearing in the CAF 'Money Management' and 'How To' series are designed to provide both volunteers supporting smaller charities – in either an official or an unofficial capacity – and inexperienced salaried staff with practical information and guidance on good practice.

Money Management series

BANKING *Gail Moss*

ISBN 1-85934-094-6 £9.95

Published April 1999

With increased competition in the financial services market and the vast array of products available, it can be difficult to see how best to meet the banking requirements of voluntary organisations.

This book starts from first principles, guiding readers through the process of assessing their current banking arrangements, surveying what is available in the market, negotiating charges and monitoring banking relationships. Offering plenty of practical, hands-on advice, this book can help any treasurer achieve tailored banking arrangements which contribute to the success of their organisation.

MANAGING YOUR INVESTMENTS *Gail Moss*

ISBN 1-85934-095-4 £9.95

Published April 1999

Investment income can be crucial to a voluntary organisation being able to carry out its objectives, especially when the voluntary sector is under pressure to provide more help for beneficiaries while funding is tight. At the same time, people running organisations have a responsibility – and a legal obligation in the case of registered charities – to hold their organisation's assets in trust for those who benefit from their work, and to ensure the assets are well looked after for future generations. This means that voluntary organisations need their investments to provide a good return whilst managing their money with great caution.

This book guides readers through the sophisticated investment market in a straightforward way. It gives a clear overview of what investment products and services are available and offers advice on how organisations can get the return they are looking for.

How To series

THE TREASURER'S HANDBOOK *Ian Caulfeild Grant*

ISBN 1-85934-018-0 £7.95

Published August 1996

Recent legislation has reinforced the crucial role of the treasurer in voluntary organisations of all sizes, whilst the introduction of the SORP is intended to lead to a greater uniformity of practice throughout the sector.

As a treasurer's duties become more onerous, their personal, legal liability for the 'prudent management' of their organisation is thrown sharply into relief. Yet many volunteer treasurers do not have even a basic understanding of bookkeeping activities.

In straightforward language, avoiding financial jargon, *The Treasurer's Handbook* outlines a treasurer's key tasks, proposes appropriate procedures and explains the basics of financial management.

PAYROLL GIVING *Willemina Bell in association with Penny Clover*

ISBN 1-85934-061-X £7.95

Published June 1998

Payroll giving provides a regular, dependable income for an organisation by enabling employees to contribute to a cause of their choice through their employer's payroll. The results can be continuing income, new friends and donors and access to a host of other fundraising opportunities.

In a practical, easy-to follow way this guide shows readers how to make payroll giving work for their organisation, explaining in straightforward terms how payroll giving works and giving advice on how to recognise opportunities and how to run successful meetings with employers and employees.

APPLYING TO A GRANT MAKING TRUST A GUIDE FOR FUNDRAISERS *Anne Villemur*

ISBN 1-85934-033-4 £7.95

Published February 1997

Grant making trusts of all sizes complain that many of the funding applications they receive fail either to match their stated funding priorities or to provide a coherent explanation of the project or programme for which support is being sought. Consequently, they are not eligible for consideration.

In response to this situation, and drawing on the author's years of experience as editor of the Directory of Grant Making Trusts, this book provides step by step guidance in drawing up a well-rounded 'case for support' which contains all the information that trustees require when considering an application.

Index

additional costs 73, 74–75, 76
advice, obtaining:
  financial 26, 27–28, 58
  legal 34
affinity borrowing 15–16, 53–55
affinity saving and lending schemes 16
agreements, loan 29–30, 78–79, 80–81
  renegotiating 81
arrangement fees 73, 76
assessments, financial 35–36
asset finance 14–15
assets as security 19–22
  legal aspects 32–34
Aston Reinvestment Trust 50–51, 85

Banking Ombudsman 83–84, 88
banks (*see also* lenders) 48–49, 56–57
  affinity borrowing 15–16, 53–55
  getting information on 57–58
  location 66, 67
  relationship with staff 67
  soft lending 18
book debts 21
borrowing communities 17–18, 55
borrowing limits 42, 69–70
borrowing restrictions 29–30
bridging loans 8, 16, 37, 44, 77
  repayment periods 43
building projects, financing 12
  see also properties
building societies 49
  Ecology 52
  Nationwide 49, 85
Building Societies Ombudsman 84, 88
'bullet' capital repayments 13, 73
Business Moneyfacts 58, 86
business plans 43–44, 59
businesses, information on 48

CAF *see* Charities Aid Foundation
'cap and collar' loans 72
capital, repaying *see* repayments
capital allowances, claiming 14, 15
cars *see* vehicles
cash flow forecasts 40–42, 44, 60
Central Young Men's Christian Association 38–39
'charges' (on assets) 19, 32–33
  fixed 33
  floating 21, 33
  on property 19, 20, 33
charitable trusts *see* trusts
Charities Aid Foundation 51, 90
  Investors in Society 51, 52, 85
Charity Commission 24, 86
  booklets 27, 28, 89
  justifying decisions to borrow 24–26
  obtaining approval from 26–27
Charity Times 34, 57, 58, 86
Charity World 57, 87
Churches National Housing Coalition 54–55
Co-operative Bank, The 53
Co-operative Finance Housing Society 85
complaints, making 83–84
'connected persons' 26, 28
costs *see* interest rates
  additional 73, 74–75, 76
covenants 29, 80
credit checks 78
crystallisation events 33

debentures, mortgage 33
debts:
  factoring and invoice discounting 13–14
  as form of security 21
default interest 75
defaulting 82
  and disposal of assets 32, 33–34
  legal aspects 30–32
deposit-taking 18
'drawdown' facilities 12

Ecology Building Society 52, 85
Employee Ownership Loan Fund
Scotland 85
equipment as security 20–21
EU contracts: as security 21
euro loans 43
extending loans 42, 81

factoring services 13–14
Factors & Discounters Association
14, 87
Finance & Leasing Association 15,
87
financial advice, obtaining 26,
27–28, 58
financial assessments, making 35–36
Financial Services Act 17
Financial Services Authority 17, 18,
87
fixed charges 33
floating charges 21, 33
foundations, loans from 49–50
freehold property 20
FSA *see* Financial Services
Authority

Glasgow Regeneration Fund 85
governing documents 23–24, 77
guarantee communities 16–17, 55

Hastings Trust 51–52
'heads of terms' 78
hire purchase 14, 15
housing associations 49, 65
Housing Finance Corporation, The 85

income and expenditure *see* cash flow
forecasts
Industrial Common Ownership
Finance 85
information, obtaining:
on lenders 48, 57–58
see also advice
insolvency 32
insurance:
keyman 65, 80
property 29, 80
interest, rolled-up 74–75
interest rates 12
fixed 72, 80
Libor 71
negotiating 72–73
on overdrafts 11
variable 42–43, 71, 72, 75, 80
intermediaries, social investment
50–55, 85
investments as security 22
Investors in Society *see* Charities Aid
Foundation
invoice discounting services 13–14

Just Housing Account 54–55

leasehold property 20
leasing assets 14, 15
legal issues/requirements:
advice 34
borrowing 12, 23–30
defaulting 30–32
mortgages 27, 34
pledging security 32–34, 73
lenders 56–57
approaching 58–59
documentation required by 76–77
information needed by 59–61, 78,
79
interviewing 59, 61–65
outline offers from 78–79
problems with 83–84
researching 48, 57–58
shortlisting 59, 66, 75–76
see also banks; building societies
liabilities:
contracting out of 31–32
limited 30
unlimited 30–31
Libor (London Inter-Bank Offered
Rate) 71
'limited liability' 30
'loan-to-value ratios' 20
loans 12
alternatives to 8, 36
assessing need for 35–38
extending 42, 81
restrictions 29–30

secured and unsecured 19
security checks and controls 45–46
size required 39–43, 45
'soft' 18
when to take out 44–45
Local Investment Fund 85
lump sum capital repayments 13, 73

machinery as security 20–21
magazines, specialist 57–58
management, importance of 78
meetings with lenders 59, 61, 62–65
money laundering 46
mortgage debentures 33
mortgages 8, 33, 37, 77
legal requirements 27, 34

Nationwide Building Society 49
NatWest Bank: Community Bond 54, 85
NGO Finance 34, 57, 58, 88
'non-utilisation' fees 75

offers, outline 78–79
office equipment as security 20–21
Ombudsmen:
Banking 83–84, 88
Building Societies 84, 88
overdrafts 11–12
and powers to borrow 23
unauthorised 45

'Partnership' accounts 54–55
penalties, early repayment 43, 73
plans, business 43–44, 59
'pledges, negative and positive' 29–30
powers to borrow 23–24, 77
properties:
converting 73, 77
insuring 29, 80
purchasing 12, 25–26, 37, 38–39, 51–52
as security for loan 19, 20, 33, 62, 70, 75, 79
see also mortgages
provident societies 30

Radical Routes 85
receivers, appointment of 82
renegotiation of terms 42, 81
repayments 12–13
and borrowing limits 42, 69–70
'bullet' 13, 73
calculating costs 70–73
flexible 74, 76
methods 73–74
period required 43, 73
see also defaulting; interest rates
rolled-up interest 74–75
Royal Charter, organisations with 23, 30

secured loans 19
security, assets as *see* assets
security checks and controls 45–46
segregation of duties 46
Shared Interest Society 85
shares as security 22
signatories, authorised 45
social investment intermediaries 50–55, 85
'soft' lending 18
solicitors 34
stock market investments as security 22

trading companies 14, 29
Triodos Bank 16, 53, 55, 85
trusts:
loans from 48, 49–50
trustees' liabilities 30–32, 46

unauthorised borrowing 45–46
unincorporated organisations 30–31
and liability 31–32
Unity Trust Bank 53
'unlimited liability' 30–31
unsecured loans 19

vehicles:
hire purchase 14, 15
as security for loan 21